CW01468489

Heroic Struggle
Bitter Defeat

Heroic Struggle

Bitter Defeat

Factors Contributing to the Dismantling of the Socialist State in the Soviet Union

Bahman Azad

International Publishers
New York

© International Publishers, New York

First Edition, 2000

All Rights Reserved

Library of Congress Cataloging-in-Publication Data

Azad, Bahman.
   Heroic struggle!—bitter defeat : factors contributing to
the dismantling of the socialist state in the Soviet Union /
Bahman Azad.
      p. cm.
   Includes index.
   ISBN 0-7178-0726-6
   1. Communism—Soviet Union—History. I. Title
HX311.5 .A96 2000
947.084—dc21

                                                    00-040729

Printed in Canada

Contents:

Foreword   *11*

Introduction:
Eighty Years After the Victory of the
Great October Socialist Revolution   **17**

1. The Great October Revolution and the Achievements
   of Socialism   17
2. Global Consequences of the Dismantling of the
   Socialist Camp   22
   • "New World Order"   23
3. The Need for a Correct Assessment of the Past Errors   29

Part One:
Some Methodological and Theoretical Considerations   33
1. On the Question of Methods   33
2. Theoretical Foundations of Scientific Critique of
   the Existing Socialism   37
3. On the Question of Models   41
   • Historical Approach to Socialist Models   46
4. Socialism from Theoretical Point of View   48
   • Socialism as a New Type of Society   48
   • "First Phase" of Communism and the Dynamics
     of its Development   50
   • (a) Relation Between the Party and the State   55
   • (b) Relation Between the Party and the Class   58
   • (c) Relation Between the State and the Class   62
     — Bourgeois Democracy vs. Socialist Democracy   62

Part Two:
**The Objective/External Factors Contributing
to the Crisis of Socialism**   **71**

1. The Initial Level of Development of Productive Forces   73
2. Building Socialism Under the Siege of Imperialism   76
   • The "War Communism" Model (1918-1921)   77
   • The "New Economic Policy" (NEP) Model
     (1921-1928)   81
   • The "Rapid Industrialization" Model
     (1928-1945)   86
3. The Destructive Effects of Fascist Aggression   98
4. Cold War and the Arms Race   101

Part Three:
**The Subjective/Internal Factors Contributing
to the Crisis of Socialism**   **105**

1. The "Rapid Consumption Growth Model" and the
   Grounds for Economic Crisis   108
2. The "Advanced Socialism Model" and the Grounds
   for Political Crisis   118
   • Priorities of Economic Planning   121
   • The "State of the Entire People"   124
   • The "Party of the Entire People"   128
3. Socialism, Imperialism and World Revolution   132
4. Proletarian Internationalism and the Relationship
   Among the Parties   140

Part Four:
From Renewal to Dismantling of Socialism   **147**

1. The Initial Phase of Transformations   147
2. The 27th Congress: Boosting Socialism's Potential
   for Development   154
3. From Correction to Total Destruction—
   Gorbachev's "Humane Socialism" Model   158

Conclusions:
Was the Collapse Inevitable? 171

- The Role of "New Thinking" 174
- Lack of Resolute Response by Communists 176
- The Future 180

Afterword 183
Index 187

Heroic Struggle
Bitter Defeat

Foreword

My original research on the historical process of socialist construction in the USSR dates back to the mid-1970s, when I was a doctoral student of sociology and economics. As a Marxist sociologist with a special focus on social change and comparative economic systems, I was engaged in studying the process of socialist development — especially economic development — in the USSR. Indeed, it was my academic research and in-depth exposure to the tremendous economic and social achievements of socialism in the Soviet Union that transformed me from a simple Marxist academician into a dedicated activist for the cause of socialism and Communism — a dedication that has continued to define every aspect of my life up to the present day.

My initial academic approach to the question of socialist construction kept my fascination with socialism's historic achievements from blinding my eyes to the difficulties — both theoretical and practical — that existed in the path of the development of socialism in the USSR. My years of study on the subject had taught me that this was neither an easy task nor a short-term struggle. Moreover, my studies had shown me that what existed in the USSR was not a perfect society, as many of us used to think at the time, but a transitional society struggling to overcome internal and external obstacles in its path to perfection. Indeed, it was an

incomplete social system with many shortcomings and deficiencies; while still being the best that human civilization
had produced through centuries of economic, social, cultural
and scientific development. I came to see the flaws of the
existing socialist systems in the same light as one sees the
flaws of a Boeing 747, or those of the Apollo mission to the
moon, or those of the Space Shuttle today: They all point to
the present limits of humanity's achievements; they all must
be overcome if human civilization is to advance beyond where
it is today. I came to realize that the existing socialist systems
were to be defended, not because they were flawless ideal
systems, but because they constituted the height of humanity's
historical achievements; because they were, and still are, humanity's only way to a peaceful, prosperous future.

Indeed, it was this rational understanding of socialism's
historical necessity that helped me maintain my emotional
balance in the face of the shockwaves that followed the dismantling of the socialist states in the Soviet Union and other
European countries. The loss of these socialist systems led
me not to disillusionment and despair, but to the logical
question as to why and how such a historical setback and
reversal had become possible?

That is why I wholeheartedly some of my colleagues'
suggestion that I should write an essay on the possible causes
of the dismantling of the socialist state in the Soviet Union.
This time, however, the task was quite different. While in
the 1970s my research was primarily focused on the oft-
ignored and systematically downplayed historical achievements of the existing socialist countries, this time the main
task was to look for the faintest signs of potential problems
in the same volume of historical material that had earlier
proved the superiority of socialism over capitalism.

In order to achieve this, I had to constantly keep in
mind several important methodological points. First, given
the tremendous emotional impact of the destruction of the
socialist states on progressive people and especially on Com-

munists, it was imperative that I avoided falling into the trap of negativism and rejectionism toward the past that some had already fallen into. My first concern, therefore, was to not allow the prevailing negative emotions get in the way of rational historical analysis.

The second point was to keep in mind the enormous historical dimensions of the process of socialist construction as well as those of the recent setbacks, and thus avoid making sweeping generalizations — positive or negative — based on mere experiences of a given party, group of people, or even a generation. The process of socialist construction that started with the great October Socialist Revolution encompassed the whole world and involved over one hundred Communist and Workers' Parties. The evaluation of its historical achievments and failures, therefore, could not be carried out in a comprehensive manner unless the experiences of all these parties and nations — especially those of the CPSU and the People of the Soviet Union — were gathered, analyzed and incorporated into the analysis. Such a tremendous task requires an enormous amount of resources, and cannot be achieved in a short period of time — not at least within the life time of one single generation. As a result, one has to refrain from making hasty judgments and ahistorical generalizations that are merely based on immediate experiences.

Third, and probably my most important methodological concern, was to avoid losing sight of the interests of the working class in this difficult endeavor. The immediate danger in carrying out such a task lies in the fact that one can easily mistake one's own subconscious class interests and worldview for those of the working class as a whole, thus leaving the doors open for the substitution of an objective, working-class analysis of socialism's past with a broad bourgeois attack on socialism and Communism.

This book was written with these serious, methodological concerns in mind. I must therefore emphasize here that it is being presented as neither a comprehensive nor a conclusive account of socialism's past achievements and failures in the USSR. Rather, it must be seen merely as a simple effort, another spring board, for launching a much needed and long overdue concrete discussion of the factors that contributed to the dismantling of socialism in the USSR and eastern Europe.

Finally, a few points must be mentioned about the content of this book. First, as it was mentioned earlier, most of the historical data presented in this book are based on the research I had done during the decades of the '70s and '80s. They are primarily taken from Western sources that, as a matter of course, over-emphasized the shortcomings and under-emphasized the historical achievements of socialism in the USSR. Although these could be replaced with more accurate data provided by socialist sources, including the government of Soviet Union, I decided against doing so. My primary reason was to let the reader read about the achievements of socialism from Western sources rather than from the Communists themselves. In my view, these Western confessions to socialism's tremendous achievements, albeit under-emphasized, are quite revealing in themselves.

Second, most of the conclusions drawn herein are based on prolonged discussions with my colleagues and comrades, some of whom hold differing views about the relative importance of one or another factor involved in the dismantling of the socialist state in the USSR. Although I am greatly indebted to all of them for their insights and contributions, I am solely responsible for the arguments and conclusions presented in this book.

Third, I am greatly indebted to two of my comrades — whose names I cannot, unfortunately, reveal — for helping me in the final editing of portions of this document.

Last but not least, I am deeply grateful to those comrades who encouraged me to transform and publish this document as a book.

I dedicate this work to Comrade Gus Hall for his revolutionary leadership; to the memory of the late comrade, Michael Davidow, for his uncompromising internationalism; and to the living memory of the late comrade Noureddin Kianouri, who dedicated his whole life to the cause of Socialism and the working class.

Bahman Azad
May 2000

Introduction:

Eighty Years After the Victory of the Great October Socialist Revolution

1. The Great October Revolution and the Achievements of Socialism

Our world, at the beginning of the 21st Century, has gone through tremendous and surprising transformations. The process which began with the Great October Socialist Revolution over eighty years ago and which, through the establishment of the first workers' state in the world, profoundly affected the course of development of human history, has now entered a new stage due to the dismantling of the Soviet Union and other socialist states in Eastern Europe.

During the past century, the idea of socialism was extensively spread throughout the world. Within a short period of time, developing socialism succeeded in eliminating poverty, hunger, unemployment, homelessness, and lack of access to health and education in a vast area of the globe. Following the October Revolution, Soviet society took gigantic steps toward industrialization and economic development and, within the span of less than three decades, transformed itself from an underdeveloped capitalist country into an advanced industrial society, and an economic power second only to the United States.

With the establishment of socialist ownership of the means of production, the peoples of the Soviet Union and later other socialist countries achieved a number of unprecedented rights and liberties. The working people in these countries were guaranteed the right to work, the right to shelter and housing, the right to free healthcare and education, to social security, and the right to benefit freely from various cultural and artistic services provided by the socialist society — rights that were, and still are, virtually unimaginable in most capitalist countries.

Socialism immediately recognized full equal rights for women in its constitutional laws — rights which, even at the end of the 20th Century, are not fully implemented in a great many of the advanced capitalist countries. The Soviet state systematically facilitated women's active participation in the economy and guaranteed equal pay for equal work. By the mid-1980s, women in the socialist state, the Soviet Union, constituted over 51 percent of the society's active workforce. In many economic fields women were far ahead of men: they constituted 75 percent of doctors and healthcare workers, 73 percent of teachers, 70 percent of cultural workers, 76 percent of the trade sector workers and 68 percent of communications workers in the Soviet Union. In order to further facilitate women's participation in the workforce and their active involvement in all areas of social life, the socialist society systematically provided women with such services as childcare at the workplace, generous maternity leave, shorter work days and workweeks for working mothers, and even arrangements for working at home while raising infants. Although the centuries-old heritage of women's oppression, and especially the backwardness of Russian society at the turn of the 20th Century, kept women's condition far from what it could have been in an "ideal" socialist society, nevertheless, one can confidently claim that the historic achievements of socialism in the area of women's emancipation were both unprecedented and undeniable.

18

The establishment of socialism and the recognition of the equal rights of nationalities by the socialist state created the most favorable conditions for fraternal and peaceful co-existence of all nations throughout the Soviet Union, and later in other multi-national socialist countries. Throughout the whole period of socialist rule in these countries, different nationalities, despite all their cultural and social differences, and despite previous conflicts among some of them, lived side by side in a peaceful and internationalist manner. By eliminating the material conditions that give rise to national conflicts, and by guaranteeing the welfare of all, socialism proved that animosities and conflicts among nations arise not from cultural differences among them, but from poverty, underdevelopment and the economic and political competition that emerges due to competition for resources. The revival of wars and national conflicts in these countries following the dismantling of the socialist states is vivid proof of this fact.

The October Revolution acted as the trigger for a process that led to the collapse of the old colonial order in the world. With the help of the socialist camp, the old colonial system was removed from the face of the Earth, and many "third world" countries obtained their political and, to some degree, their economic independence.

During WWII, the forces of socialism, first and foremost the Soviet Union, played a determining role in defeating the menace of fascism, thus saving the human race from the danger that threatened its future existence. Due to the increasing prestige of socialism, which was a direct result of its internal achievements as well as its role in the victory over fascism, the national liberation struggles in many countries took a socialist orientation. In some countries, like China, Cuba, Vietnam, Korea, etc., socialist revolutions succeeded. The selfless economic, political and military aid provided by the Soviet Union played a significant role in these countries' economic development and social progress. The socialist revolution in Cuba, which imperialism is still trying to brutally destroy, is a living and undeniable example of such socialist achievement.

During the period following WWII, socialism played an important role in securing world peace and preventing inter-imperialist rivalries from turning into destructive wars. During the post-WWII period alone, the Soviet Union and other socialist countries presented to the world community over 160 proposals for disarmament, nuclear test bans, and even unilateral nuclear arms reduction — all of which were ignored by the imperialist powers. The Soviet Union's move in 1985 toward a unilateral nuclear arms reduction despite the serious threats that this could involve for its national security, and the Soviet proposal for a nuclear-arms free world by the year 2000, are still shining examples of the socialist countries' efforts to safeguard world peace and eliminate tensions from international relations. These efforts created tremendous prestige and respect for socialism among the peace-loving peoples of the world.

The successes, and the increased material and moral authority of socialism in the world, had a significant impact on the economic, political and social life in capitalist countries. The achievements of socialism along with the struggles of workers in capitalist countries, forced the ruling classes in these countries to make extra concessions to the working people in order to prevent the spread of socialist thought and the Communist movement among workers. Throughout the capitalist world, the right to organize labor and trade unions as well as the right to collective bargaining for workers was recognized. The labor movement in capitalist countries, in most cases benefiting from the international strength of socialism, reached new heights and forced significant economic and social reforms upon the capitalist order. In the United States, the labor movement, aided by the Communist Party, USA, succeeded in forcing a universal social security and unemployment compensation system upon the ruling class. In Western Europe, the labor movement directly entered the political arena and, in the form of social democracy, forced significant changes in the political superstructure of the capitalist system, carrying out major reforms in the mode of exchange in these societies. In many capitalist countries, social democracy became the predominant form of organization of the political life. The economic and social gains of the working class in many capitalist countries have now become an integral part of the objective reality, and the ruling classes in these countries are facing serious difficulties and fierce resistance by the working class in their efforts to take them back.

One of the most significant and irreversible global achievements of socialism has been its impact on extending and deepening the meaning of the concept of fundamental human rights. The example of socialist countries extended the concept of basic human rights to also include such economic rights as the right to work, the right to housing, the right to healthcare, the right to education, and such principles as peace and social justice as the most universal rights of all human beings. This extended meaning of the concept of human rights, which has been embraced by the great majority the people throughout the world, was based on and inspired by the practical achievements of socialist societies. Today, securing these rights constitutes the most fundamental and irreversible demand of the people throughout the world — a demand that is incompatible with the essence of the capitalist system under which they live.

The October revolution and the emergence of socialist systems in the world opened a new chapter in the history of human society, the full impact of which has not yet been fully realized. Despite all the difficulties faced by the existing socialist countries due to various objective and subjective factors, socialism has now proven its inevitability — as well as its superiority over the capitalist system — beyond any doubt. The inevitability of socialism arises out of the inner

21

essence and the contradictory nature of the capitalist system itself, and no temporary setback, regardless of how disastrous it may be, can refute this inevitability.

2. Global Consequences of the Dismantling of the Socialist Camp

The historical setback caused by the dismantling of socialist states in the Soviet Union and other Eastern European countries was a disaster not only for the Communists, the working class and the people of these countries, but for humanity as a whole. As a result, the achievements of the new human civilization during the past eighty years, and the fruits of the selfless work and sacrifices of several generations of working people in socialist countries to build and defend their new type of society, were trampled upon by the class enemies of the working class.

The working people of these countries, after decades of self-sacrifice, were expecting improvements in their standard of living and the quality of their economic, political and social life, and were sincerely attempting to redress the shortcomings of the socialist order in their countries. They were suddenly confronted with a rising tide of poverty, hunger, inflation, unemployment, homelessness, prostitution, corruption, organized crime, national conflicts, civil wars, partition of their motherlands, political and military coups and, worst of all, domination of imperialist governments and their international institutions over all economic, political, social and military life of their society.

The true dimensions of this disaster have now become evident to all, including the working people in former socialist countries. It has now become clear, as the increasing strength of Communists in these countries demonstrates, that this setback was not something that the millions of working people

22

in socialist countries had desired. Rather, it was the outcome of the interaction between a number of objective and subjective factors, including mistakes and deviations that occurred in the course of the construction of socialism; constant plots, interventions and sabotages that were carried out by imperialist states against socialist countries; and, ultimately, the betrayal of socialism by a number of Party and government leaders and officials in socialist states. It is self-evident that a comprehensive and scientific assessment of the role of these factors is needed to overcome the present setbacks.

"New World Order"

The consequences of the present setback go far beyond the borders of the former socialist countries. The dismantling of the socialist states in the Soviet Union and other Eastern European countries has temporarily changed the balance of class forces, both globally and in each individual country, in favor of pro-imperialist reactionary classes and forces, and against the exploited and oppressed classes and democratic and patriotic movements. What is being imposed on the peoples of the world by imperialism, and especially by U.S. imperialism, as the "new world order" today, is nothing but an open manifestation of this negative shift in the balance of class and social forces on a world scale.

The basic features of this "new world order" are: a universal increase in the level of military, political and economic aggression and intervention by imperialist states in the internal affairs of other countries; increased freedom for the transnational monopolies in the unchecked plundering of the defenseless peoples of the "third world;" increasing transformation of such international bodies as the UN Security Councilinto subservient instruments of imperialist oppression and exploitation throughout the world; more open and defiant use of force in international relations by imperialist states —

both militarily in the form of invasion and occupation of other countries, and economically in the form of imposing economic sanctions and trade embargoes — intensification and in many cases conscious instigation of national, ethnic and religious conflicts and confrontations around the world with the purpose of partitioning and dismembering countries of strategic and economic importance and imposing unrestrained imperialist domination over them — as seen so clearly in the dismembering of Yugoslavia. In short, violation of political independence, national sovereignty and the territorial integrity of all countries, especially those of "third world" nations, with the sole objective of securing absolute domination of the transnational corporations and imperialist states upon them. This constitutes the principal characteristic of the "new world order" that has emerged.

With the dismantling of the socialist bloc and especially the Soviet Union, the working and oppressed peoples of the "third world" lost their staunchest international supporter in their struggles against imperialism.

The governments of many of these countries, which had previously achieved a relative degree of "nonalignment" and independence from the West with the help of Soviet Union and other socialist countries, are now being crushed under intense and unilateral pressures from imperialism, conceding to ever-increasing concessions to the imperialist states and transnational corporations.

The national liberation movements in various counties, having lost an important ally, are now increasingly forced to either retreat from their original national and anti-imperialist objectives or face direct military assaults by imperialist states.

The United Nations, which until recently constituted a platform for "third world" countries to express their demands and exert collective pressure on imperialism and, to a certain degree, isolate the imperialist states with the help of Soviet Union's veto power in the Security Council, is being increasingly pressured by the imperialist powers to act as a force against the "third world" countries and oppressed nations, national liberation movements and the revolutionary forces throughout the world.

The loss of the socialist camp, which provided economic support for the countries trying to break away from the international cycle of capital, has severely limited the options of many "third world" nations in adopting socioeconomic models for their development that are free from the yoke of international capital. The global and absolute domination and control of the imperialist states and transnational corporations over all sources of finance and investment capital, and their monopolized control over the world market, has enabled them to use their unchallenged economic power to isolate, defeat, and if necessary directly crush, any attempt in the "third world" countries to pursue an independent, non-capitalist development path.

Today, the imperialist states are using every means at their disposal, especially their "neoliberal" economic policies — privatization, elimination of the public sector, imposition of open-door trade policies, removal of all forms of government planning of the economy, elimination of all forms of state subsidies, compensations and social protections, etc. — to crack open the economies of the "third world" countries and pave the way for a complete penetration by international capital and transnational corporations. The objective of these policies, which are being forcefully carried out by such international imperialist institutions as the World Bank and the IMF, is to intensify and expedite the flow of surplus value into the advanced capitalist centers. Without a doubt, the logical outcome of such a policy is an increased plundering of the natural and human resources of these nations, blockage of the process of capital formation in their national economies, a total halt and even reversal of the course of their economic development, a drastic drop in their standard of living, and, in general, an ever-increasing level of poverty, disease, deprivation and homelessness among the great majority of the world population.

The temporary shift in the world balance of forces in favor of imperialism, however, does not mean the emergence of a "unipolar" world dominated by "super-imperialism" as a unified, coherent force. The inner objective contradictions of the capitalist system in its imperialist stage were neither a result of the emergence of socialist states on the world scene, nor have they disappeared as result of the dismantling of some of these states. On the contrary, every evidence points to the fact that these contradictions have intensified and assumed new and broader dimensions. Imperialist states, especially U.S. imperialism, have imposed tremendous costs and suffering upon their own people in their decades-long quest to destroy socialism in the world. Unprecedented levels of poverty, disease, hunger, malnutrition, unemployment, inflation and deterioration of the people's standard of living in many advanced capitalist countries is a direct result of the squandering of a large portion of their material and human resources for the purposes of military confrontation, the nuclear arms race, cold war propaganda, and espionage and sabotage against the socialist countries, national liberation struggles and the Communist and working-class movements throughout the world. The economic bankruptcies and astronomical budget deficits caused by these policies, along with the intensification of class contradictions during the past several decades, have intensified the economic and social crises in these imperialist countries. To alleviate these crises, the imperialist economies will need astronomical levels of capital accumulation and concentration. And this is at the time when the imperialist powers must meet a greatly increased financial burden in their efforts to prop up and maintain pro-capitalist, pro-West governments in the former socialist societies.

On the other hand, the dismantling of the socialist bloc has not only removed a unifying factor among the rival imperialist states, but has also boosted inter-imperialist rivalries over who takes the lion's share of the "spoils" of the post-cold war period. Such aims as expanding their own "areas of influence," exporting their economic crises to other countries, forestalling others' efforts to control the weaker nations' natural and human resources and their domestic markets, and installing puppet regimes that would serve one imperialist power at the expense of its rivals, have now taken a more prominent place in each and every imperialist state's agenda. The emergence of three major imperialist blocks led by the United States (NAFTA), Germany (Maastricht) and Japan (in Southeast Asia), and the increased competition among these three blocks for extending their areas of influence in the world by means of instigating civil, national and regional conflicts and wars, is vivid proof of increased inter-imperialist rivalries.

Considering the problems that are confronting the imperialist countries today — intensified class contradictions and social conflicts, deepening economic and financial crises, and increased inter-imperialist rivalries — one can expect that, from a historical perspective, the present negative shift in the world balance of forces in favor of imperialism is only temporary and transitional. The global contradiction between labor and capital; the contradiction between a handful of imperialist states and the rest of humanity; the ever-widening gap between wealth and poverty in the world, which increasingly manifests itself in the gap between over-production by transnational monopolies, on the one hand, and lack of purchasing power for these same products among the great majority of the world population, on the other; the economic bankruptcy of a great majority of the "third world" countries and their inability to repay their heavy international debts — all these are increasingly causing great problems for the financial and banking systems of the imperialist countries. The loss of credibility and the ever-increasing economic and political bankruptcy of "social democratic" policies aimed at "resolving" the problems and contradictions of the capitalist system from within the system itself has led to a continuous shift of the social democrats to the right, the ascendancy of various right-wing bourgeois parties to power, revocation of most social protection plans, and the widening gap between the rich and the poor in all of the advanced capitalist countries.

The disastrous economic condition and the poor standard of living of the great majority of people in the former socialist countries and their growing awareness of the anti-human and exploitative nature of the capitalist system is increasingly manifesting itself in the election of former Communists and even present supporters of socialism to power. Finally, the intensifying environmental crisis that has led the wasteful and polluting capitalist system to a virtual dead-end — all point to the transitional nature of the present situation and the inevitability of the re-emergence of a powerful anti-capitalist, anti-imperialist pole, albeit in a new form, on the world scale.

Fully aware of the transitional and temporary nature of the present balance of forces in the world, imperialism is doing its best to take advantage of this short historical opportunity to strengthen its positions and remove every government or force that would in any shape or form resist the rapid implementation of its "new world order." This policy is being pursued globally at three different levels: weakening and/or overthrowing the remaining socialist states in the world (China, Cuba, Vietnam, North Korea, Laos...); rapid "resolution" of the international conflicts and problems facing imperialism through the imposition of unequal and unbalanced agreements on social and national movements which have been weakened as a result of the dismantling of the socialist camp (as in Palestine, South Africa, Ireland, etc.); and suppressing, invading, partitioning, or weakening those governments and countries that, for whatever reason or purpose, refuse to submit to imperialism's "new world order."

The military operations that are being carried out around world today under the guise of such international institutions

as the United Nations and in the name of "providing human-
itarian aid," "defending world peace," "safeguarding human
rights," and "upholding democracy," are all an integral part
of the imperialist powers' general strategy of consolidating
their absolute domination over the world before this short-
lived transitional stage is passed.

3. The Need for a Correct Assessment of the Past Errors

The speed of destruction of the socialist states and the
dimensions of disaster resulting from it were so huge that it
created a great amount of confusion not only among the
working class and people of the socialist countries but also in
the world Communist movement. A hasty search for the
"principal cause" of this historic setback began immediately.
Imperialism mobilized its propaganda machine to proclaim
the "death of Communism," "end of socialism," and "final
victory of capitalism." The intensified imperialist propaganda,
combined with the slanderous attacks waged from within
the Communist movement by Gorbachev and his cohorts
against socialism, Marxism-Leninism, the history of the
CPSU, and the world Communist movement, paved the
way for all sorts of incorrect "theoretical criticisms" of socialism and the ideal of Communism. Accusation, falsification
and slander were substituted for responsible scientific analysis.
An overall ideological attack on socialism and its achievements
commenced.

The enemies of the working class attempted to present
these setbacks as "proof" of the futility and impracticality of
socialism and a confirmation of their claim that in the absence
of the profit motive and capitalist market no social progress
is possible. Gorbachevite and non-Gorbachevite social democrats used this setback as a staging platform for renewed
attacks on Marxism-Leninism in general and on Lenin's the-

29

ories on imperialism in particular. They tried to separate Marx from Lenin and prove that Leninism constituted a philosophical and theoretical deviation from Marxism, and not an adaptation and elaboration of this theory and philosophy for the age of imperialism, as is commonly believed. According to them, the crisis in socialism had started not with Stalin, as some claimed, but with Leninism and Lenin himself. Others, who can be said to be under the influence of bourgeois-liberal ideology, claimed that people's yearning for a Western-style, bourgeois democracy was the main cause of crisis in socialist countries: i.e., the people's inability to "vote" and "directly elect" their leaders. In their view, such a crisis would not have emerged if people were given a chance to enjoy participation in a parliamentary bourgeois democracy.

The significance of this historic setback, combined with imperialism's barrage of anti-Communist propaganda and the outpouring of such superficial "analyses," had its effects on Communists as well, and led to the development of serious theoretical and non-theoretical disagreements within the Communist movement itself. Disillusioned by the setback, some decided to walk away from the struggle. Others, including some Communist and workers parties, changed course, rejecting Marxism-Leninism and the class struggle, and joining the ranks of social democratic and reformist parties. In response to this change of course, some leaders and members of these Parties, who did not believe in such changes in their Party's orientation, gathered together and formed their own Marxist-Leninist Party.

The Parties that insisted on maintaining their Marxist Leninist course were not immune to such conflicts either. In many of these parties, some leaders tried to separate themselves from the past history of socialism and the policies of the Communist movement. They focused their criticisms on the Communist Parties of the former socialist countries, and particularly on the CPSU and its leadership. Within this tendency, some opportunistically turned against their own Party leadership, accusing them of being an "accessory" to "Stalinist crimes." This approach, which was mainly adopted for the purpose of exonerating one's self and blaming others for the past mistakes, thus substituted the Leninist principle of "self-criticism" with the opportunistic method of "criticizing others." In many cases, this approach ended up in personal slandering of Party leaders, factional activities and ultimately splitting from these Parties.

At the opposite end, such ideological attacks and unscientific methods led some Communists to put forth an unconditional defense of everything that existed in the past, equating principled defense of Marxism-Leninism with justification of past mistakes, blaming the setback solely on external factors and imperialist intrigues. In this manner, the line of demarcation between ideological-scientific issues and the past performance of the existing socialist countries was blurred and scientific analysis gave way to polemical arguments.

The after effects of this theoretical anarchy, disillusionment, confusion and disunity are evident, although for some time now many of these issues have been clarified.

Today, many of the Communist Parties have resolved these issues and have re-established their firm commitment to Marxism-Leninism. Nevertheless, for the Communist and working-class movement to regain its past strength and resume its leadership position in the struggles to overcome the present situation, it must be able to produce a comprehensive and convincing analysis of the causes and factors that have been responsible for this historic setback. Many Parties have responded to this historical necessity by taking very important and valuable steps in the direction of producing such an analysis.

Communists are fully aware of the fact that providing a comprehensive analysis of the causes of the present setback is a task that can be done only through a collective effort of all Communist and workers parties throughout the world, espe-

31

cially in collaboration with the Communist and workers parties which were directly involved in the process of construction of socialism. This is a long-term project which can neither be left to a few individuals or parties, nor be confined to predetermined timetables.

For this reason, this book is one attempt to shed some light on certain aspects of this very complex historical process. The most important element in this attempt has been strict adherence to scientific method, without losing sight of working-class partisanship. This principle is a necessary foundation for an objective and scientific assessment of socialism's historical past.

Part One

Some Methodological and Theoretical Considerations

1. On the Question of Methods

Any evaluation of socialism's past, to be a responsible one, must be carried out with scientific honesty. This means that such an assessment must, before anything else, clearly define and declare its premises and assumptions, and openly state its biases. Only on the basis of its stated premises and assumptions can such assessment be judged scientifically. Otherwise, contention over socialism's past can easily diminish into empty polemic and subjective rhetoric.

It is for this very reason that strict adherence to Marx's dialectical method in the study of human history and society is necessary, the most important principles of which are specified in his "Introduction" to *A Contribution to the Critique of Political Economy*. Two of these principles constitute the foundation of any scientific study of human history and society.

The first principle, as emphasized by Marx, is that in any scientific study,

> [t]he subject, society, must always be envisaged ... as a
> pre-condition of comprehension even when the theoretical

method is employed.[1]

Marx means that when studying a social phenomenon, one must, before anything else, be fully aware of the nature of the epoch and society he or she is living in and, hence, of the nature of the biases this particular epoch and society has etched upon his or her mind and reasoning. Moreover, one must recognize his/her own ideological and class position within the society and clarify the class position from which he or she is studying the phenomena.

In Marx's view, our understanding of social phenomena is scientific when it is based on the worldview of the most progressive class of our epoch, i.e., the working class, and its most advanced political organization. Such a worldview will best enable us to understand the essence of our epoch and the nature of the historical stage in which we live in its totality, and to determine the role and place of each and every phenomenon within this totality. What results from this process is a unified collection of scientific concepts that guide us in our scientific understanding of the existing reality. Concepts developed on the basis of the dialectical and historical materialist worldview and the struggles of the proletariat during the past 150 years are examples of such effective theoretical and scientific tools. It is true, of course, that such concepts, too, need to be reviewed, sharpened and further elaborated in light of the recent developments. But it is also clear that such a task can be achieved only within the framework of the scientific worldview of the working class as the most progressive class of our times with the objective of advancing the historical interests of the working class as a whole.

The significance of this principle lies in the fact that for an assessment of socialism's past record to be scientific, it

---

[1] Karl Marx, *A Contribution to the Crtitique of Political Economy*, International Publishers, New York, 1970, p. 207.

cannot be based on bourgeois-democratic intellectualism. Nor can it be based on petty-bourgeois sensationalism and romanticism or perfectionist idealism. Rather, such assessment must start out from the materialist class outlook of the international working class and its leading political parties. Adoption of such an outlook, however, cannot be done through a mere "study" of the views and positions of the proletariat, but through an objective and practical rejection of all non-working class outlooks and continuous implementation of the principle of self-criticism in the course of active participation in the struggles of the working class on a world scale. Without a direct linkage with the practice of class struggle, any assessment of socialism's internal processes is reduced to a mere intellectual exercise within the limits set by the dominant bourgeois worldview.

Thus, direct involvement in the class struggle of the proletariat and a constant, critical correction of its path during the course of struggle is the only correct method for a scientific assessment of the past and a successful resolution of the present crisis. Addressing the past problems of socialism from any other vantage point would certainly be marred with the subjective prejudices of bourgeois society and, hence, would deprive us of any objective assessment of reality.

The second methodological principle set forth by Marx is the recognition of the fact that

> ... even the most abstract categories, despite their validity in all epochs — precisely because they are abstractions — are equally a product of historical conditions even in the specific form of abstractions, and they retain their full validity only for and within the framework of these conditions.[2]

This means that social or natural phenomena cannot be

---

[2] *Ibid.*, p. 210.

treated as a static, independent collection of fixed qualities, but as dynamic moments in the totality of social and natural relations in the course of their historical development; and for this reason, their essence and qualities change and acquire a new meaning in direct relationship to the contradictions of each historical stage. Hence, no phenomenon can be scientifically analyzed in isolation from its ontological ground and the historical circumstances and contradictions that have given rise to it. On the contrary, Marx's scientific method requires that all social phenomena (including the present models of socialism, democracy, Party, "Stalinism," etc.) be analyzed within the framework and in direct relationship with the contradictions of the specific historical stage that constitutes its logical ground.

Thus, to achieve a scientific assessment of a phenomenon, one must start, not from a compilation of "self-evident" local and partial truths, but from a general understanding of the most universal contradictions of the objective reality surrounding the phenomenon. In other words, such a study would start from the most general (most objective and complex) aspects of reality, and then progressively narrow down its focus on more particular elements of the reality. The critical consideration in this process is that, at each level, the effects of the more general on the more particular phenomena must be carefully analyzed and integrated into the analysis, so that each particular phenomenon is analyzed as an integral part of its dialectical ground and not as an isolated, individual case. For example, from a scientific point of view, one cannot begin one's critique of the past models of socialism with a critique of such phenomenon as "Stalinism." This is because a correct understanding of a phenomenon such as "Stalinism" requires an understanding of the internal Party processes; this, in turn, requires an understanding of the relationship between the Party and the working class; this latter requires an understanding of the internal structures of the socialist formation at each stage; this, in turn, requires an understanding of the existing social and historical contradictions of the system which, in turn, requires an understanding of the more general contradictions on a world scale. Thus, Marxist methodology dictates that this process be carried out in the reverse order.

These principles constitute the essential difference between a dialectical and dynamic approach and a static, abstract one. A scientific investigation of the kind that has been placed on the Communist movement's agenda today must inevitably base itself on these methodological principles.

2. Theoretical Foundations of A Scientific Critique of Existing Socialism

It has become fashionable in various circles today for every criticism of socialism's past to start with the premise of the "invalidity of the past theories." Unfortunately, this phenomenon manifests itself not only in anti- and non-Communist literature but also among some Marxist thinkers as well.

The generalizations about the "invalidity of the past theories," meaning Marxism-Leninism, have no scientific basis: It is not clear in what way the "past theories" have lost their validity or: where lie the signs of such a loss of validity. If the claim is based on the emergence of the crisis in socialist countries, then the task would be to investigate the historical roots of the crisis, to distinguish between the subjective and objective factors responsible for its emergence, and then, to isolate and review those elements from among the subjective factors that are theoretically based. None of these tasks have so far been carried out systematically, and as a result, claims about the theoretical roots of the present crisis are premature and devoid of scientific support.

Second, even if one assumes that such a task has been

accomplished, the results should show which parts and aspects of the "past theories" — which assumptions, arguments, conclusions, and most importantly, theories pertaining to what aspects of the objective reality — have been incorrect and therefore invalid? Is Marx's theory of surplus value invalid? Are the analyses of the contradictions of the capitalist system incorrect? Is Lenin's theory of imperialism incompatible with reality? Is the theory of the vanguard party of the proletariat defective? Are the theories about the path of socialist construction faulty?...

It is quite clear that sweeping generalizations about the "invalidity of past theories" are tantamount to a negation of all these and hundreds of other theories that constitute the component parts of the Marxist-Leninist worldview. Such generalizations, which completely ignore the diversity and complexity of the "past theories" of Marxism-Leninism, can in no way be considered scientific statements.

Class analysis of the stages of development of human society toward socialism and communism; the discovery of human "labor" as the central and determining element in shaping the course of development of human society; formulation of the concepts of "exploitation" and "surplus value" as scientific tools for understanding the capitalist mode of production; identification of the proletariat as the "grave-digger" of the capitalist system and the motor force for socialist revolution; and dozens upon dozens of other complex ideas and theories have not merely been subjective creations of isolated minds. Nor can they be discarded at will, without regard to their organic relationship with objective reality. These concepts and theories about present-day social systems, which constitute the foundations of scientific socialism, have been developed through a dialectical application of scientific methodology to the study of human society, and can be rejected only through the use of the same scientific methodology.

Third, the principles of dialectical thought teach that no

phenomenon appears or dies by itself. This is especially true in the process of scientific production. The history of science has proved over and over that "past theories" have, always and without exception, been rejected only after the emergence of, and by means of advancing, new theories. No scientific theory has ever lost its validity without being rejected by a newer, more scientific one. The loss of validity of a theory can be proved by its inability to explain the existing or the newly emerged phenomena. By the same token, the loss of validity of Marxism-Leninism, as a body of scientific theories, can be proved when its inability to explain the new phenomena has been demonstrated. So far, no one has been able to provide such a proof, and thus to claim that, for the first time in the whole history of science, Marxism-Leninism has been refuted in the absence of a newer theory is to fly in the face of the whole history of scientific practice.

There is no doubt that such claims of the "invalidity of Marxism-Leninism" are based solely on negative developments in Socialist countries during the past decade. The dismantling of the Socialist states in the Soviet Union and other Eastern European countries, people's mass demonstrations and protests against the shortcomings and economic problems, and the revival of the capitalist market economy in these countries, are all being presented as the "proof" of "the invalidity of Marxism-Leninism." In other words, mere observation of a series of specific historical events in a specific period of time and in a specific number of countries is used as a justification for such broad theoretical generalizations. Even worse, these generalizations do not stop at the level of hypotheses and theory, but are extended into the realm of philosophy and ideology without any consideration for the logical and historical context in which these phenomena have emerged. Such a method of deduction is not only unacceptable in any field of science today, but was proved unscientific by both Marx and Engels more than a century ago.

Those who declare the "invalidity of Marxism-Leninism"

without putting forth a newer, more scientific theory are, consciously or unconsciously, serving only one purpose: reviving the older, pre-Marxist theories and justifying the old order that is based on these theories. In the present conditions, the only guide and compass for Communists in their efforts to overcome the past problems and chart a new course for socialism is Marxism-Leninism as the most revolutionary science of the day. Without such a scientific theory, any assessment of the past events loses its class base and therefore its objectivity, and is bound to end up in the abyss of opportunism.

It is true that recent developments in certain Socialist countries have necessitated a re-evaluation of some of the past concepts and practices. But this by no means implies the "invalidity" of Marxism-Leninism as a worldview, as an ideology and as a scientific outlook. Class struggle, as an objective reality and an integral part of the dialectical process of history, continues independently of our subjective state of mind, and will continue until the establishment of the Communist society. In this struggle, Marxism-Leninism, as the most progressive and most scientific worldview, constitutes the most effective means for the correction of past errors, and for the liberation of humankind from exploitation and oppression.

The theoretical foundations of socialist construction may require some changes. But these changes are needed only in the direction of their expansion and refinement in light of the new experiences and conditions. We should not forget that at the end of the last century, Lenin, too, was faced with a similar task. He succeeded in paving the future course of the movement not by declaring the "invalidity" of Marx's and Engels' theoretical concepts, but by building upon their theories, and refining and expanding their concepts so they corresponded more precisely with the realities of class struggle in the era of imperialism. Such is the task that history has once again put before Communists.

3. On the Question of Models

We are confronted with similar abstract generalizations with regard to the issue of models of socialist development. Many Marxist thinkers, while defending Marxism-Leninism and the theories of scientific socialism, seek the causes of the present setbacks in the "failure of the 80-year-old *model* of socialism." Such an approach, in our view, is also afflicted with serious problems that need to be analyzed.

Such a claim, before anything else, assumes the existence of a single general model for socialism not only in different countries of the world, but also within a single country such as the Soviet Union. This assumption, however, can be proven incorrect both theoretically and historically. But the greatest inconsistency in this line of reasoning, even when applied to a single country like the Soviet Union, lies in the fact that it counterposes the "theory of socialism" to its "model" in reality.

From a theoretical point of view, when we speak of the success or failure of a socioeconomic model, we must first determine which theoretical premises constitute the foundation of this model, in what historical context has the model emerged, which contradictions and historical necessities have given rise to it, and what historical and social objectives it has been designed to achieve. It is quite clear that the success or failure of any model can only be judged with reference to its goals and the objective conditions in which it has sought to achieve these goals.

What makes the issue more complicated is the existence of external factors and their impact on the success or failure of a socioeconomic model. The fact is that no socioeconomic model emerges and develops in vacuum. Both the existing contradictions on a world scale and the past and present socio-historical contradictions within the society itself, play a role in the success or failure of any model at each stage of

41

its development.

To all these one must add another determining factor, namely, the performance of the vanguard Party that is charged with the historical responsibility of implementing and advancing that model within the society. This, in turn, depends on the level of the vanguard's understanding, experience, and degree of it adherence to the theoretical and scientific premises of the model, on the one hand, and its ability to adapt the general requirements of the model to the specific objective and subjective conditions that prevail in society at each stage of its development, on the other.

With all these factors in mind, it becomes quite clear that the determination of the success or failure of a model, if it is to be done responsibly, cannot be based on abstract generalizations. Rather, it requires the deepest possible investigation and understanding of the historical, social, economic, political and even cultural features of the society in which the model has been implemented.

To prove the failure of a model, therefore, one must be able to demonstrate that the model's inability to achieve its objective has been neither the result of the impact of external factors, nor of the invalidity of its theoretical premises, nor of mistakes made by the social vanguard, but of the insurmountable structural contradictions within the model itself. In other words, it must be demonstrated that the model in question has failed, and would have necessarily failed, due to its own internal contradictions, regardless of the impact of all other external factors. Only then can one speak of the failure of the model and search for a "better" one.

Such a determination, as far as we know, has not been made with regard to "the 80-year-old model of socialism." Nor have the first steps in this direction even been taken by the world Communist movement. The sole basis for such a claim at this point in time seems to be the general disillusionment that has grown as a result of the present historical setback in some socialist countries. But, in the absence of a more scientific worldview, theory and model, and given the fact the no class struggle can be advanced without a revolutionary theory and a socioeconomic model to guide it, a premature claim to the "failure of the 80-year-old model of Socialism" is tantamount to calling upon the working class to relinquish its struggle for socialism until the time when a "better," "more scientific" worldview and socioeconomic model has been "discovered."

There is yet another important and alarming consequence arising from such a line of reasoning. When we speak of the "*theory* of socialism," we are in fact talking about something pertaining to certain aspects of *objective reality*. No theory can be defined as a mere conceptualization of an *ideal*. Socialism was transformed from a utopian *ideal* into a scientific *theory* by Marx and Engels exactly when they demonstrated the possibility and the inevitability of its existence *in reality* through the discovery of the laws of motion of historical materialism and the class struggle. It was thus that Socialism was transformed from "utopian" into "scientific."

Furthermore, in a second step in 1917, this "ideal" of socialism was once more transformed, this time from the realm of *scientific theory* — from a possibility — into *actual reality*. The October Revolution and the creation of the first socialist state transformed socialism into a reality that has not only affected the lives of millions of people around the world, but has also left its irreversible marks of achievement on the entirety of modern human history — the objective history of humankind. The fact that socialism, in spite of all its deficiencies, has existed in the past 80 years, at the very least establishes a certain correspondence between the theory and practice of socialism. Now, to reduce the *reality* that has existed for the past 80 years into a mere *theory*, and not only that, but to argue that this "theory" has even failed to produce the material proof of its validity during the past hundred years, means taking not one, but two steps backwards in history. It is, in fact, an implicit claim to the invalidity of the *theory* of socialism itself.

Today, after 80 years of actual history of socialism, any attempt to separate its theory from its practice is bound to deny the very theories that real existing socialism has been based on. It is tantamount to saying that socialism has never existed except in the form of an "ideal." It is tantamount to regressing back into "utopian" socialism. It is a way of conceding defeat while at the same time clinging on to some vague hope for an unknown future.

We have all heard from many good-hearted people, including liberals and elements of the bourgeois class itself, that "socialism is very nice in theory, but not practical in reality." This latter argument goes only one logical step beyond the thesis of the "failure of the 80-year-old model of socialism" — a step which the proponents of this thesis may never want to take, but many others are eager and willing to take out of their own sense of defeat. This is the ultimate danger that lurks behind such an argument.

But the class enemies who eagerly embrace the thesis about the "failure of the 80-year-old model of socialism" are no utopians. On the contrary, they are very clear about the existing reality and know very well what they want to do with it. Unlike new, disillusioned utopians, they are not out to *deny* the existence of socialism in the *past*; they want to prevent its continued existence in the *future*. They are out to convince the working people that *socialism has indeed existed in the past* and that its very existence in reality has proven its *unavoidable* "inherent flaws" — flaws that make it even worse than capitalism itself and thus devoid of any future. Zbignew Brzezinski has best described the essence of the "inherent flaws of socialism" thesis:

> The fatal dilemma [read: flaw] of Communism in the Soviet Union is that its economic success can only be purchased at the cost of political instability, while its political

stability can be sustained only at the cost of economic failure.[3]

Had this been meant to be a *theoretical* criticism, its advocates would have engaged in proving that socialism, just like capitalism, has systemic contradictions within its infrastructure; that the socialist relations of production, by their very nature, inhibit the growth and development of the productive forces of society; that the basic principles of the socialist mode of production — public ownership of the means of production, planned economy, internationalism, and above all, the principle of "from each according to their ability, to each according to their contribution" — are self-contradictory and impossible to apply. They refuse to engage in such an effort not because they are not interested in such a proof, but because they know very well that they will not be able to prove such absurd claims.

It is quite clear that here we are not dealing with a theoretical rejection, but a *political-ideological attack* on socialism; an attack which is aimed not only at the destruction of real existing socialism but at socialism as a "theory" and even an "ideal." For this very reason, the "failure" thesis cannot simply be seen as a purely *theoretical* debate about socialism's past weaknesses, but as an integral part of the *continuing attack on the future of socialism*.

We are able to carry out an historic task in defense of socialism successfully only based on objective realism and avoid puritanism and utopianism. The fact is that, "no new society ... came into being and developed bloodlessly and free of mistakes and crimes,"[4] and in this regard, socialism's 80-year-old history could not have been an exception. The task, therefore, is not one of discarding the "faulty" socialism of the past and creating a new "flawless" socialism for the

---

[3] Gus Hall, *The Power of Ideology*, New York: New Outlook Publishers, 1989, p. 27.

[4] Gus Hall, *Political Affairs*, August 1992, p. 3.

45

future, but that of improving, developing and guaranteeing the future of the very real, existing socialism — *the one and only* socialism, with all its achievements and shortcomings — that has existed in human history since 1917, and continues to exist today. As the founders of scientific socialism themselves emphasized:

> Communism is for us not a *state of affairs* which is to be established, an ideal to which reality [will] have to adjust itself. We call communism the *real* movement which abolishes the present state of things. The conditions of this movement result from the premises now in existence.[5]

Historical Approach to Socialist Models

The principal defect of the "failure of the 80-year-old model of socialism" thesis is its *ahistorical* approach to the question of socioeconomic "models" in socialist countries. Such an approach is a clear violation of the basic principles of Marxist scientific methodology. The fact is, during the 75-year history of the Soviet Union there was not just a single "model" of socialism, but several successive "models" which were devised at various historical stages in response to both internal and international developments, and the need to achieve different socioeconomic objectives. Nor can we claim that we have been dealing with models of "socialism" as conceptualized in theory, but rather, with various "models" of "transition to full-fledged socialism," as the Soviet leadership and the country's various Constitutions would testify. These were "models" for the transition of a *particular* society, with its *unique* historical characteristics, toward the stage of "advanced socialism."

Thus, the first answer that such a thesis must provide is

---

[5] Karl Marx and Frederick Engels, *The German Ideology*, International Publishers, New York, pp. 356-7; *Marx Engels Collected Works*, Vol. 5, p. 49.

which "model of socialism" is it referring to? The initial "War Communism" model? Stalin's "rapid industrialization" model? Khrushchev's agricultural and consumer-goods model? Brezhnev's "mature socialism" model? Or, Gorbachev's "democratic and humane socialism" model? Have all these models pursued the same objectives? Have all of them equally failed or succeeded in achieving their objectives? Have all of them equally been in violation of the basic premises of the theory of socialism? And finally, have all of them been equally responsible for the ultimate demise of the socialist order in the Soviet Union? It can be seen very clearly how such ahistorical generalizations can obscure, rather than clarify, the fundamental questions before us, thus hindering the true process of scientific investigation of the problems.

For this reason, one must resolutely reject such ahistorical approaches to the past history of Socialism, and insist on a truly historical approach — as proposed by Marx — which examines each stage of the development of socialist society within its proper historical context and in reference to its designated objectives. Only thus can one determine the degree of success or failure of a specific model, the degree of its adherence to the basic principles of socialism, and its historical contribution to the quantitative and qualitative development of socialist society in the long run. Such an approach would allow us to trace, both structurally and chronologically, the logical and historical roots of the problems that contributed to the ultimate dismantling of these systems. It will help us to isolate the specific policies or measures that were responsible for the emergence of certain problems at any particular stage, and to determine the objective or subjective, super- or infra-structural, internal or external, nature, as well as the degree of inevitability of each of the emerging problems. Only then, can we truly discover the real causes of, and the logical and historical relationships between, the numerous contributing factors. Clearly, this is a gigantic task. But it is an unavoidable one which, more than anything else, requires patience, hard

47

work, a true sense of responsibility, and strict adherence to scientific principles.

4. Socialism from A Theoretical Point of View

Any sincere effort to assess the shortcomings of the past models of socialism must, before anything else, define and clarify the theoretical premises that constitute its foundation. In other words, such an assessment must inevitably be based on a clear theoretical understanding of the general principles that govern socialism and its internal structures. Since theoretical notions of socialism and historical expectations from socialist systems have been different even among most serious Marxist thinkers, it is necessary to first clarify the theoretical conception of Scientific Socialism and the principles that are guiding us in this discussion.

Socialism as a New Type of Society

As a new type of society, socialism is governed by certain general laws as outlined by Marx in his materialist conception of history. Some of these general laws are universally applicable to all modes of production, and some apply to socialism alone.

According to Marx, all modes of production, without exception, consist of an economic infrastructure (objective element) and a superstructure (subjective element). The economic infrastructure of the mode of production, according to Marx, consists of relations of production (relations of ownership of the means of production) and forces of production (labor, knowledge, tools and technology, land, etc.). The superstructure, on the other hand, consists of all political, ideological, cultural, philosophical and other such structures that emerge out of this economic foundation. In all modes of production, the superstructural elements operate within the constraints set by the economic infrastructure and are "conditioned" by this infrastructure. Mutually, these superstructural elements are capable of influencing infrastructural elements and processes within the mode of production. Again, in all modes of production, the dominant superstructural elements, especially the political structure of the state, are at the service of the ruling classes, helping maintain and reproduce the existing relations of production in accordance with the interests of the ruling classes. Finally, in all modes of production, the dominant relations of production, while shaped by the level of development of the productive forces at any given time, in turn guarantee and facilitate a certain degree of growth of these productive forces within the limits set by the interests of the ruling classes.

From a historical point of view, in all modes of production, there comes a time when the quantitative growth of the forces of production surpasses the limits set by the dominant relations of production and thus necessitates a change in these relations. At this stage, the intensifying conflict between the forces of production and relations of production leads to a social revolution and the establishment of a new set of relations of production that are compatible with the new level of development of the productive forces of society. In this manner, the new relations of production replace the old ones and the process of growth and development of the forces of production continues within the framework of the new relations established by the new order. This historical process is characteristic of all modes of production, including socialism.

In class societies, however, due to the presence of the exploiting classes who find the preservation the existing relations of production in their own class interest, this process of replacement of the old by the new is confronted with special complications and contradictions. Here, the ruling classes and the political structures set up by them, especially the state, act as a brake on the process of renewal of the relations of production. As a result, the process of substitution of the old by the new always necessitates a social revolution that overcomes the resistance put forth by the ruling classes and their state. This is the most important feature that distinguishes all previous class-based societies from the new socialist society.

From the Marxist point of view, the working class, by eliminating all forms of class exploitation and all exploiting classes, removes all obstacles from the natural path of substitution of the old by the new and thus guarantees the continuous growth and development of society's forces of production. With the elimination of the exploiting classes, a major driving force for the preservation of the status quo also disappears from society and the relations of production are allowed to assume a fluid, constantly changing character. That is why Marx considers Communism not as a specific "mode of production" or a specific "stage" in the historical development of human society, but as a constant process of "abolition of the present state of things." Thus, from a historical-materialist perspective, what distinguishes a developing socialist society from all previous class-based societies is its fluid and constantly changing relations of production that allow for a continuous and uninterrupted growth and development of society's productive forces. This unique feature is what makes socialism a new type of society and separates it from all previous societies in human history. This feature also constitutes the most fundamental criterion by which the adequacy and health of the past models of socialism must be judged and assessed.

"First Phase" of Communism and the Dynamics of its Development

Obviously, one cannot approach Marx's concept of a Communist society in an abstract and idealistic manner. As Marx emphasized in his *Critique of the Gotha Programme*, socialism as the "primitive phase" or the "first phase" of Communist society has certain characteristic features that set it apart, both structurally and qualitatively, from Communism. In his description of the "first phase" of Communist society Marx wrote:

> What we have to deal with here is a communist society, not as it has *developed* on its own foundations, but, on the contrary, just as it *emerges* from the capitalist society; which is thus in every respect, economically, morally and intellectually, still stamped with the birth marks of the old society from whose womb it emerges.[6]

What are these "birth marks"? First is that human beings in such a society still carry with them all subjective and objective characteristics and limitations that they inherited from capitalism — including personal greed, lack of class consciousness, social prejudices, much mis-education and limited knowledge, etc. Second, the productive forces of the society have not yet reached the level of development that is necessary for satisfying all material and cultural needs of the people. Hence, the Communist principle of "to each according to their needs" cannot be realized in the first phase. Third, due to the differences that exist in the abilities and capabilities of individual producers, the principal of equality among all members of the society, which is one of the fundamental features of a developed Communist society, cannot be recognized as an objective for the socialist society in its early stages of development. Indeed, not only is the principle of "to each according to their contribution," which guides the process of distribution of goods and services under socialism, based on inequality among producers, but it in fact intentionally promotes such inequality. And there is a historical and scientific reason for this.

---

[6] Karl Marx, *Critique of the Gotha Programme*, International Publishers, New York, 1938, p. 56.

The socialist principle "to each according their contribution" not only makes socially useful labor the only source of income for all members of society, but also aligns the private interests of producers with the social goal of uninterrupted growth of the forces of production. At the same time, what is returned to the producers in the form of wages compensates them for only a portion of what they have produced for society. The remainder of the value produced by workers is turned into public property by the state and is deposited in society's "public fund." It is, therefore, quite clear that in the early phases of Communist society not only does the exploitation of human labor (not in the form of class exploitation, of course) continue in a socialist process of production, but is indeed consciously intensified. The Socialist State, acting on behalf of society as a whole, constantly tries to increase the level of production and maximize the sum total of surplus value generated throughout society by creating material incentives for more work and superior performance.

This planned inequality through wage differentiation is the most important and effective means for a socialist society to increase labor productivity and guarantee continuous growth of the forces of production during its early phases of development. Obviously, conscious utilization of the most advanced scientific and technological achievements of human society constitutes an integral part of this planned process.

The qualitative difference between this planned inequality within the socialist system and the inequality that characterizes the capitalist mode of production lies in the public appropriation of the surplus value generated under socialism. This surplus, after some deductions for such socially necessary expenses as the administration of the state, maintenance of public order, etc., is transferred to a "social consumption fund" and is used for improving the living standards of society as a whole, and for providing social services for all members of the society in a universal and equal manner without any regard to the quantity or quality of their work.

It is here, and not at the level of production, that the Communist principle of "to each according to their needs" is at work from the very first phases of socialist development. However, it is quite clear that the growth of this communist sector of the socialist society is directly linked to, and its realization depends on, the development of the productive forces and a continuous growth in the amount of surplus value generated in the productive sector of the economy. In other words, the growth of the communist sector within the womb of the socialist economy is a direct function of the development of its forces of production and of the continuous increase in the productivity of labor in the sphere of production.

In this manner, each member of a socialist society benefits from the material resources of the society in two distinct ways: First, through direct wages that one receives in accordance with the quality and quantity of work performed for society; and second, free social services and benefits that are provided universally, regardless of one's amount of work for the society. The sum total of direct wages and free services thus received constitute one's total income under socialism. Naturally, in the early phases of the development of socialism, when the forces of production are less developed and material incentives, not communist consciousness, constitute people's primary motivation for work, wages constitute the most important part of workers' income and their main motive for performing socially useful work. But as socialist society develops, the share of communist benefits and services received by the workers increases relative to the share of direct wages in their total income. Thus, with the continuous development of socialism, as the relative share of free, universal benefits grow in workers' total income, society gradually moves away from the principle "to each according to their contribution" and approximates the Communist principle of "to each according to their needs."

These elementary concepts are crucial to the continuous

and uninterrupted development of a socialist society towards Communism. Lack of proper attention to these issues can disrupt the process of socialist development, hinder the growth of its forces of production, and ultimately lead to a crisis in the system.

1. Socialist production, by its very essence and its historical mission, is absolutely incompatible with the levelling of wages. Indeed, socialism would be able to achieve its long-term objectives only through a well-planned system of wage differentiation. Any attempt towards a mechanical levelling of wages can only result in the weakening and destruction of material incentives that are vital to increasing labor productivity under socialism. Lack of attention to this critical principle on the part of the leading Party and planners of socialist society, and especially, a premature application of advanced Communist principles to the early phases of socialist development — or "rushing ahead" as Marx called it — can be detrimental to the process of socialist production.

2. Even in the advanced phases of socialist development, this principle remains valid. Communist equality will be realized not by removing material incentives from the sphere of production but as a result of the continuous growth of the "social consumption fund," to a point where the amount of workers' direct wages becomes totally insignificant as compared to the value of free social benefits and services they receive from society. Indeed, the most important measure of a socialist society's growth and development, and degree of its advancement towards Communism, is the ratio of the value of producers' free benefits and services to the amount of direct wages in their total income. No political decision or subjectively defined criterion can replace this objective measure.

3. A mere quantitative growth in a socialist society's surplus product cannot by itself be taken as a measure of its advancement towards Communism. The measure must also be defined in terms of how this surplus product is allocated;

to what degree it is put to productive use; and to what extent it has been used to elevate the living standards of the producers themselves. Miscalculations in social and economic planning; mismanagement and misappropriation of the surplus product; increasing channeling of the surplus product into such non-productive areas as state bureaucracy, military expenditures, wars, corruption, etc., can derail the process of socialist development and hinder society's historical march towards Communism.

The Role of the Subjective Factor in Socialism: (a) Relation between the Party and State

Uninterrupted growth of the forces of production under socialism is a result of yet another feature that distinguishes socialism from all previous societies. Marx describes this distinguishing feature as follows:

> Communism differs from all previous movements in that it overturns the basis of all earlier relations of production and intercourse, and for the first time consciously treats all naturally evolved premises as the creations of hitherto existing men, strips them of their natural character and subjugates them to the power of the united individuals. Its organization is, therefore, essentially economic, the material production of the conditions of this unity.... The reality which Communism creates is precisely the basis for rendering it impossible that anything should exist independently of individuals, insofar as reality is nevertheless only a product of the preceding intercourse of individuals.[7]

Thus, Communism involves not only a total elimination of class exploitation from human society, but also a reversal of the dialectical relationship between the subjective and objective elements in society. For the first time in the history

---

[7] Karl Marx, *The German Ideology*, International Publishers, New York, 1947, p. 86; *MECW*, Vol. 5, p. 81.

of humankind, there emerges a social system in which human beings consciously subjugate socioeconomic structures of the society to their own powers and manage to put them at their service instead of being blindly driven by them. In his description of this unique feature of Communism, Marx goes even as far as rejecting the independent existence of such structures from conscious human beings.

Thus, domination of the subjective over the objective factor constitutes the second distinguishing feature of socialism and Communism. Unlike the previous class-based societies, where society's infrastructures, and above all, its property and production relations, determined the direction of the movement of subjective and superstructural elements, in a socialist society, where the means of production have become the common property of society as a whole, it is the subjective factor that consciously determines the course of movement of the infrastructure. From the Marxist-Leninist point of view, this subjective factor is no other than the working class and its political party which, after winning political power and replacing the bourgeois state apparatus, lead the socialist society towards Communism according to a consciously developed plan.

There are important reasons for the emphasis on the role of the working class and its Party here. From a theoretical perspective, there are important reasons for not confusing the vanguard role of the Party with the role of the state under socialism:

1. According to Marx's analysis, the state, under all circumstances and in all modes of production, including socialism, has the universal role of maintaining and reproducing the *existing* relations of production. Although under socialism this role implies maintenance and reproduction of *socialist* relations of production, nevertheless, the task of maintaining and reproducing the *existing* relations of production in a society that is based on the premise of constant overhaul of these relations is, in essence, a conservative and static task.

2. A socialist society is still not a classless society. The socialist state, although under the control of the working class, does not represent only the working class and its exclusive class interests. The socialist state must represent, both domestically and internationally, the interests of all working people and all classes that are present in a unified socialist society. In this sense, the concerns and responsibilities of the state, acting in accordance with the interests of the socialist society as a whole, are quite different from those of the Party, which is charged with the task of promoting the interests of the working class as the most advanced class of society. While the State is charged with the task of managing and preserving the existing socialist society as a whole, the Party has the task of moving the socialist society towards Communism by constantly transforming the present state of affairs in society.

3. From the economic point of view, the public ownership of the means of production under socialism charges the State apparatus with the responsibility of managing the socialist economy on behalf of the working class and the masses of the working people. In such circumstances, there is always an inherent danger that the state bureaucracy, given its narrow political and economic interests, will abuse its managerial control over the socialist economy to its own advantage rather than advancing the class interests of the working people. In other words, it may consider itself the employer, rather than a representative of the working people. In such a situation, the Party of the working class is faced with the peculiar task of defending and advancing the interests of the working class *vis-a-vis* the bureaucratic tendencies within the state apparatus. In most cases, this responsibility should place the Party on the side of the working class, not the state bureaucracy.

4. As Lenin has emphasized, the state apparatus in all societies, including socialism, has a bureaucratic nature and usually develops certain interests of its own that in most

cases are incompatible with the long-term interests of the working class. Workers' control over the state can by no means eliminate such incompatibility of interests. Marx emphasized that the development of Communism is characterized by a gradual withering away of the state in socialist society. Obviously, such a process cannot be left to the state bureaucracy itself. Rather, it must be carried out by the working-class Party in a conscious, well-planned manner regardless of any resistance put forth by the state bureaucracy.

For these reasons, any confusion of the role and responsibilities of the socialist state with those of the Party and even worse, any relegation of the historical tasks of the Party to the state, will have serious consequences for the process of socialist development. Any form of merger between Party and State structures would result in the growth of bureaucratism, carreerism and corruption within the ranks of the Party, weakening of the Party's vanguard role and distancing it from its class base. In the long run, such phenomena would inevitably lead a socialist system into a deep-rooted crises.

Any assessment of the past models of socialism must, therefore, include a close examination of the relations between the Party and the state in each and every stage of development of the given socialist society. Such examination must be carried out not only with regard to possible mergers between the Party and the state structures, but also in relation to the degree of the socialist state's adherence to socialist principles and the Party guidelines, as well as the Party's ability to recognize the historical requirements of each and every stage of socialist development and to propose realistic plans for advancing society towards its Communist objectives.

The Role of the Subjective Factor in Socialism: (b) Relation between the Party and the Class

From the Marxist point view, the proletariat — the working class — is the motor and its political Party is the leader of socialist revolution. From a Leninist point of view, the unity of the Party and the class is vital for the success of the socialist revolution and the forward march towards Communism. From both theoretical and historical perspectives, the unity of the Party and the class has certain preconditions that must be considered in any evaluation of the past models of socialism.

By rejecting the idea of spontaneous development of socialist consciousness among the proletariat, and by advancing the thesis that such consciousness must be brought to the proletariat by its political Party "from outside," Lenin placed the Communist Party at the core of the historical process of socialist revolution, and in doing so, relegated several important tasks to the Party. At the same time, he set Party-working class unity as the most important precondition for the success of the Party in performing its historic tasks.

The first task of the Party, Lenin emphasized, is to ideologically educate and politically organize and lead the proletariat in its daily class struggle. From an organizational point of view, the Party is responsible for gathering together all forces of the proletariat and concentrating its struggle against the bourgeoisie. In Lenin's words, the Party must be "an organization of revolutionaries capable of lending energy, stability, and continuity to the political struggle."[8] In his view, without such a Party, the masses will lack the "unity of will" necessary for leading the socialist revolution to victory. This unity of will, not only within the ranks of the workers, but also between the working class and its Party, is the key for a successful revolutionary struggle.

However, at the early stages of socialist development, when the working class has not yet achieved a high level of ideological education and class consciousness, the Party's decision-making and leadership role in the struggle are inev-

---

[8] V. I. Lenin, *What is to be Done?*, International Publishers, New York,, 1969, p. 103.

itably extremely high and even excessive. But, as the development of socialism continues and the ideological, political and scientific education of the working class grows, the line of demarcation between the Party and the class as a whole gradually vanishes and the class assumes an ever-increasing role in the Party's decision-making processes. Any disruption of this historical process of gradual but continuous transfer of the decision-making power from the Party to the class, for whatever reason, not only weakens the Party by depriving it of the knowledge and energy of the most advanced segments of the class, but also damages the unity between the Party and the class and weakens the Party's status in society as a whole.

Moreover, from an ideological point of view, the Party has the responsibility of bringing socialist consciousness to the class and translating the workers' class consciousness into political consciousness and activity. Such political consciousness, Lenin emphasized, can be achieved by the working class only through its complete understanding of the interests of, and the contradictions between, all classes in the society. In Lenin's view, such an overall understanding of class relations cannot be obtained solely from the vantage point of the working class itself. The Party must educate the working class not only in terms of its class interests but also about the interests of all other classes in society, as well as the way their interests become compatible or incompatible with those of the working class at each specific stage of class struggle. Maintaining the Party's ideological clarity and protecting it from the influence of non-working class views is a precondition for the Party's success in this endeavor.

But the Party's ideological task is not limited to educating the working class. To be able to carry out its historical mission, the Party must also place itself at the forefront of the scientific achievements of human society. As Lenin pointed out, "He who realizes how enormously the modern working-class movement has grown and branched out will understand what a reserve of theoretical forces and political (as well as revolutionary) experience is required to carry out this task."[9] Following Engels, he further stressed that class struggle involves "not two forms of great struggle ... (political and economic), ... but three," and placed "the theoretical struggle on a par with the first two."[10]

The significance of these words lies not so much in Lenin's emphasis on the important role of Marxist theory and historical materialism in class struggle, but in his emphasis on the role of the Party of the working class in the development and evolution of scientific theory in human society. And it is quite clear that such a role can be performed not by ignoring the historical achievements of human society in the area of science and technology, especially those of capitalist society, but by expanding and building upon these achievements. In other words, it is the historical responsibility of the Party to liberate human science and technology from the yoke of capitalist relations of production and turn them into assets that serve the interests of the working class.

Thus, from a Leninist point of view, in addition to the task of leading the working class in its political class struggle, the Party is also charged with the historical responsibility of revolutionary appropriation of the most advanced achievements of bourgeois science and technology, and the transformation of these achievements into effective means for the workers in their struggle against the exploiting classes. In this sense, the Party's historical role expands far beyond the liberation of the proletariat itself and encompasses the liberation of human science and technology as well.

Any delay or procrastination in this important area of class struggle, which Lenin correctly placed on par with the economic and political aspects of the struggle, can drastically reduce the Party's ability to advance socialist society towards

---

[9] *Ibid.*, p. 26.

[10] *Ibid.* p. 27.

Communism and would thus weaken and seriously damage its relationship with the class as a whole. For this reason, an assessment of the past performance of socialist societies must also include an examination of the Party's performance with regard to these principles.

Socialist Democracy:
(c) Relation Between the State and the Class

Today in many circles, including among certain segments of the left, the argument is being advanced that the dismantling of the socialist states was due to the lack of "democracy" in the former socialist countries. Bourgeois thinkers go so far as to claim that the socialist state, by its very nature, is "dictatorial" and is therefore incompatible with principles of democracy and democratic freedoms. The latter position, however, is primarily founded on the premise that the socialist state has a "monopolized" control over the means of production in a socialist society, and is therefore vested with "too much" economic, and hence, political and social power over the masses of people.

Although the two positions differ slightly with regard to the nature of their criticism of the socialist state — the first being a historical criticism and the second a theoretical one — they both suffer from a common fundamental flaw of lacking a class approach to the concepts of state, democracy and dictatorship. It is therefore necessary to elaborate on the class nature of these concepts before addressing the question of socialist democracy and the relation between the socialist state and the working class from the historical point of view.

Bourgeois Democracy vs. Socialist Democracy

Marx has clearly demonstrated that the State in any society, be it capitalist or socialist, is the principal instrument of class domination and rule. Hence, from a Marxist point of view, we are dealing not with "democracy in general" but with specific types of democracy, namely, *capitalist* democracy and *socialist* democracy. Lenin described the essential difference between the two types of democracy in a succinct way:

> Bourgeois democracy confined itself to proclaiming formal rights equally applicable to all citizens... But in reality, both administrative practices and particularly the economic bondage of the working people always made it impossible for them, under bourgeois democracy, to make wide use of these rights and liberties.
>
> By contrast, proletarian or Soviet democracy, instead of the formal proclamation of rights and liberties, guarantees them in practice first and foremost to those classes of the population who were oppressed by capitalism....
>
> The task of the Russian Communist Party is to draw ever wider masses of the working people into the exercise of their democratic rights and liberties, and to extend the material possibilities for this.[11]

Elsewhere, in the "Draft Programme of the R.C.P. (B)" [Russian Communist Party (Bolshevik)], Lenin outlined the integral elements of socialist democracy as follows:

> The historical task that has fallen to the lot of the Soviet Republic, a new type of state that is transitional until the state disappears altogether, is the following.
>
> (1) The creation and development of universal mass organizations of precisely those classes that are oppressed under capitalism.... Only in this way is it possible to ensure democracy for the great majority of the population (the working people), i.e., actual participation in the administration, in contrast to the actual administration of the state mainly by members of the bourgeois classes....
>
> (2) The Soviet system of state administration gives certain

---

[11] "Draft Third Clause of the General Political Section of the Programme (For the Programme Committee of the Eight Party Congress," March 1919, Lenin, *Collected Works*, Vol. 36, p. 505.

actual advantage to ... the urban industrial proletariat. This advantage must be used systematically and unswervingly to counteract the narrow guild and narrow trade interests that capitalism fostered among the workers and which split them into competitive groups....

(3) Bourgeois democracy ... deceived the masses with the idea that the equality of exploiters and exploited is possible. The Soviet organization of the state destroys this deception and this hypocrisy by the implementation of real democracy, i.e., the real equality of all working people, and by excluding the exploiters from the category of members of society possessing full rights.... [*see footnote, p. 62 — Azad]

(4) The more direct influence of the working masses on state structure and administration — i.e., a higher form of democracy — is also effected under the Soviet type of state, first, by the electoral procedure and the possibility of holding elections more frequently, and also by conditions for re-election and for the recall of deputies....

(5) Secondly, by making the economic, industrial unit (factory) and not a territorial division the primary electoral unit and the nucleus of the state structure under Soviet power....

(8) Soviet state organization alone has enabled the proletarian revolution to smash the old bourgeois state apparatus.... those strongholds of bureaucracy which everywhere ... has always kept the state bound to the interests of landowners and capitalists, have been destroyed.... The struggle against the state bureaucracy, however, is certainly not over in our country.... The continuation of the struggle against the bureaucracy, therefore, is absolutely necessary, is imperative, to ensure the success of future socialist development.

(9) Work in this field is closely connected with the implementation of the chief historical purpose of Soviet power, i.e., to advance toward final abolition of the state, and should consist of the following. First, every member of a Soviet must, without fail, do a certain job of the state administration; secondly, these jobs must be consistently changed so they embrace all aspects of government, all its

branches; thirdly, literally all the working population must be drawn into independent participation in the state administration by means of a series of gradual measures that are carefully selected and unfailingly implemented.

(10) ... It is precisely in making the benefits of culture, civilization and democracy really available to the working and exploited people that Soviet power sees its most important work, work which it must continue unswervingly in the future....[12]

The above passages clearly outline the fundamental elements that constitute the essence of a socialist democracy. Although the specific forms of implementation, or the degree of emphasis on each particular element of this outline may vary in different socialist societies, the principles contained in these passages are universal and can therefore be used in the assessment of the existing and past models of socialism with regard to the question of socialist democracy.

However, with regard to the question of the relation between the state and the class under socialism, a few points need to be emphasized.

---

[12] Printed on February 23, 1919, *Collected Works*, Vol. 29, pp. 105-110, 125-127.
* It is important to note here that with regard to paragraph (3) of the above passage, an "Insertion for Political Section of the Programme" has been added to the text of the Draft Programme which reads in part: "To avoid making an incorrect generalization of transient historical needs , the R.C.P. must also explain to the working people that in the Soviet Republic the disenfranchisement of a section of the citizens does not mean ... that a definite category of citizens are disenfranchised for life. It applies only to the exploiters, to those who, in violation of the fundamental laws of the socialist Soviet Republic, persist in their efforts to cling to their exploiters' status and to preserve capitalist relations. Consequently, in the Soviet Republic, on the one hand, as socialism grows daily stronger and the number of those who are objectively able to remain exploiters ... is reduced, the number of dis-enfranchised persons will automatically diminish.... On the other hand, in the very near future, the cessation of foreign invasion and the completion of the expropriation of the exploiters may, under certain circumstances, create a situation where the proletarian state will choose other methods and ... will introduce unrestricted universal suffrage."

1. Socialist democracy, as a means of guaranteeing the economic, political and social rights and freedoms of the proletariat and other working masses in a socialist society, can only be realized through upholding the interests of the working class *vis-a-vis* the exploiting classes throughout the whole process of socialist construction. As the above passages clearly demonstrate, the issue of working-class democracy under socialism is not simply a matter of "granting" the working people political and economic freedoms, but more importantly, one of guaranteeing the very existence and continued development of socialism toward Communism. The political and ideological hegemony of the working-class over the socialist state constitutes an important prerequisite for maintaining the course of socialist construction. In this sense, the working people's "direct participation in the administration of state" is not a mere exercise of democracy under socialism but a necessary guarantee for the system's integrity. Any form of weakening the working people's participation in the administration of the state is bound to open the doors for the domination of non-proletarian tendencies — the bureaucratic tendencies in particular — over the socialist state, thus diluting its proletarian outlook and diverting the whole process of socialist construction towards these non-proletarian tendencies. This, in turn, paves the way for re-emergence, growth and ultimate domination of exploitative classes and unproductive social strata and corruption in a socialist society, thus threatening the very existence of socialism itself.

2. Socialist democracy, in essence, is nothing but the application of the scientific principles of working-class organization to the society at large. It involves implementation of such principles as: collective leadership; submission of the minority to the will of the majority; submission of lower organs to the higher organs of leadership; elective nature of all organs of leadership and the masses' right to recall; and the active and effective participation of masses in all decision- and policy-making processes. Obviously, the responsibility

for the creation and expansion of material conditions for the growth and strengthening of democratic institutions and organs necessary for the implementation of these principles (e.g., unions, councils, mass organizations, etc.) lies with every socialist state. Such institutions and organs constitute the links and the bridge between the socialist state and masses of the working people. Any weakening or degradation of these institutions as mechanisms of mass participation in socialist rule, or their transformation into mere appendages of the state, not only violates the principles of socialist democracy, but also weakens the very essence of socialism. Such a process transforms the socialist state from a state of the whole class into a state of a selected elite of the class. It ruptures the link between the state and the class and eliminates the supervision of the state by the whole class, thus contributing to all forms of destructive deviations from the path of socialist construction.

3. At the same time, it is quite clear that socialist democracy, as the dominant political principle governing the process of transition from capitalism to Communism, cannot be a rigid and static principle, and must itself be transformed in accordance with the prevailing social, historical and even external objective conditions at each and every phase of the development of socialist society. In the early stages, when the antagonist and exploitative classes have not been uprooted, and especially when socialism is still under economic, political and military siege and threat from the capitalist states, socialist democracy will remain more limited in its depth and form. But as socialism develops, and as the exploiting classes increasingly disappear from society, socialist democracy expands both in depth and in form. In the absence of antagonistic classes, socialist democracy acts as the guarantor of the proletariat's political and ideological hegemony over the socialist state's structures and assumes an ever more dynamic character with the continuous development of the socialist society's productive forces.

Yet, one must not forget that the expansion of socialist democracy does not mechanically and spontaneously follow the steps of economic development in socialist society. Rather, like all other aspects of socialist society, the expansion of socialist democracy as well requires conscious planning and execution on the part of the political Party of the proletariat at every stage. Here, too, any dogmatic and rigid approach to the principle of socialist democracy, or the opposite, any subjective and voluntaristic decision for premature loosening of the class character of this principle without regard to the objective balance of class forces both within the society and on the international level, can inflict serious damages upon the process of socialist construction.

* * *

This assessment of the past performance of socialism in the USSR is based on the concepts of scientific socialism as outlined above. Each "model" of socialist society is before anything else a theoretical construct that is first devised subjectively and then implemented in reality. Therefore, its success or failure can be a result of three groups of factors:

1. The premises and theoretical foundations upon which these historical models of socialism were constructed;

2. The ability of the leading Party to correctly implement these theoretical principles, and the degree of its success in designing, implementing and adapting these models in accordance with objective, historical and social requirements of each and every stage of socialist construction;

3. The effects of the external and historical conditions under which these models were developed and implemented.

If one accepts the validity of the principles of scientific socialism as explained above, the search for the causes of the failure of the past models will primarily focus on the second and third group of factors. At the same time, there is no doubt that these two groups of factors mutually influence each other and as a result cannot be studied without regard to these mutual influences.

Communism is an international movement; its achievements and failures must be judged internationally. It is a dynamic and progressive movement that has its sights on the struggle for the liberation of humankind from class exploitation. This assessment of its past shortcomings and failures, therefore, is motivated by the desire to learn from history in order to help this great movement attain final victory for the working class and all the exploited peoples of the world.

In the final analysis, the ultimate judgment about the course of events in the former socialist countries must be left to the Communists and the parties that were directly involved in the process of socialist construction in those countries. Hence, this assessment limits itself to the most general processes and most critical issues.

Part Two:

Objective/External Factors Contributing to the Crisis of Socialism

Unlike the capitalist system whose natural course of development inherently gives rise to crises, in a socialist society it is the slowdown of growth that leads to crisis. Since each of the historical models of socialism were to guarantee the continuous growth of socialism within a given set of objective socio-historical limitations, any assessment of the degree of success or failure of each of these models must therefore be done with reference to the model's specific goals within the context of the objective limitations imposed upon it at each stage of its development.

The theory had generally predicted that the first socialist revolutions would occur in the advanced capitalist countries of Western Europe and the United States where the forces of production had attained the highest level of development and the socialist consciousness of the working class was then at a higher level. In Russia, however, theory had to adjust to reality. The fact that the first socialist revolution occurred not in the most advanced countries of the capitalist world but in the "weakest link" of the system, necessarily imposed new requirements on the process of socialist construction. Socialism started its life with a burden much heavier than anticipated theoretically and bore much more difficult responsibilities.

The first and most important of these responsibilities was to redress the objective and subjective backwardness of Russian society in relation to the other capitalist countries, as well as to create a material and productive infrastructure necessary for the establishment of socialist relations in society.

The weakness and the historical backwardness of Russian society, coupled with the superior economic and military might of the capitalist countries, allowed the latter to disrupt from the outset the growth of the socialist society through direct and indirect economic and military interferences. This, in turn, became the source of a growing defensive attitude within the socialist society, placing the "survival" of socialism at the top of the leadership's priority list. This defensive attitude played a decisive role in the development of the historical models of socialism throughout the process of socialist construction.

Another factor was the capitalist countries' economic blockade of socialism. It was the expectation of the leaders of the Socialist Revolution in Russia, including Lenin, that other proletarian revolutions would occur in the other capitalist countries of Europe, particularly in Germany, along with or soon after the October Revolution. Russia would then be able to redress quickly its economic backwardness by relying on the material and technical capability of the victorious working class in those countries. But in this case, too, the reality turned out to be different, and the young Soviet State was forced to advance its economic development solely based on its internal resources. The need to advance the socialist revolution in one country not only culminated in serious theoretical debates within the leadership of the Communist Party but also added unique features to the process of socialist construction in that country.

To these factors, one should also add the effects of World War II, the Cold War and the extensive arms race imposed on socialism after the second world war. All these factors absorbed and decimated a great part of the material and human resources of the socialist society which could have been used for developing the country's forces of production and advancing the socialist society towards Communism.

Therefore, from the beginning, the objective/external factors played a direct role in setting the general course, and conditioning the performance, of socialism in the Soviet Union. These factors, which were external to the normal functioning and historical objectives of socialism, as we shall see, played a significant role in shaping the internal processes and defining the structural features of the socialist system in the USSR.

1. The Initial Level of Development of the Productive Forces

In 1917, when the Bolsheviks took power, Russia's economic situation resembled that of many other non-developed countries. The per capita gross national product had grown a mere 9.1 percent between 1861 and 1913 (at a rate of 0.9 percent per year). This was drastically less than the comparable rates for 60 percent of the other capitalist countries at the beginning of their industrialization.[13] Over the same period, the growth rate of agricultural production in Russia was less than 2 percent annually and the growth of productivity in the agricultural sector was a meager 3 percent per decade between 1880 and 1913. Industrial production in 1913 made up only 18 percent of the economy's total production. In the same year, 72 percent of the Russian labor force worked in the agricultural sector, 18 percent in industry, and 10 percent in the service industry. In 1913, metal production

---

[13] Unless stated otherwise, all of the pre-revolution figures on the Russian economy have been drawn from Paul R. Gregory and Robert C. Stuart, *Soviet Economic Structure and Performance*, Harper and Row, New York, 1974, pp. 19-41.

made up 10 percent of the country's total industrial output and employed only 12 percent of the work force. Similar figures for other capitalist countries like England, Germany and the United States were at least double the Russian figures. In 1913, the illiteracy rate in Russia exceeded 60 percent, and the population profile of the country resembled that of Western countries *before* their industrialization. In 1913, the mortality rate in Russia was 27 per thousand, which was more than double the rate in Western Europe (13 per thousand).

Russia in 1913 was a big debtor country getting a large part of its needed capital from France, England and Belgium. The Russian economy heavily depended on foreign capital, and the low level of domestic demand was insufficient for promoting industrial growth. In 1914, foreign capital made up 20 percent of the total investment within the country. This percentage was twice that of the United States in the beginning of its industrialization in the 1880s, and 20 times that of Japan in a similar period between 1887 and 1896.

In 1917, the composition of the gross national production (GNP) in Russia was similar to that of the pre-industrialization period of Western Europe and the United States. Peasants, and not industrial workers, played the main role in the Russian economy. A large part of the population, and by the same token, of the whole workforce, was illiterate. The illiteracy rate among the large and poverty-striken peasant population was almost 100 percent. In fact, Russia in 1917 demonstrated many of the features of a "two-tier" economy characteristic of under-developed countries: an isolated, capital intensive industrial sector alongside a large, traditional and backward agricultural sector.

It was in such conditions that the Bolsheviks took power in Russia. They took steps toward building socialism in a country that, despite covering one-sixth of the surface of the Earth, was not a cohesive unit. The communication capabilities were limited; the distribution channels were incoherent; the industrial infrastructure was extremely weak and backward; the peasant economy faced tremendous problems; and the society lacked the level of social development necessary for implementation of socialist plans. The course of events after the October Revolution in Russia and later in the Soviet Union, although founded upon the conscious plans of the Communist Party for the construction of a socialist society, could not have remained immune to the direct influences of the society's culture, social composition of the population, and the past history of despotism in that country. The Russian working class thus had no choice but to first redress this immense backwardness before taking any step towards the construction of socialism. Lenin's far-sighted speech at the Seventh Extraordinary Congress of the Russian Communist Party (Bolshevik) in 1918 demonstrates this fact very vividly:

> We have just taken the first steps towards shaking off capitalism altogether and beginning the transition to socialism. We do not know and we cannot know how many stages of transition to socialism there will be. That depends on when the full-scale European socialist revolution begins and whether it will deal with its enemies and enter upon a smooth path of socialist development easily or rapidly or whether it will do so slowly. We do not know this....[14]

Thus the process of socialist construction in Russia took off from a point much further back than the theory of socialism had predicted. It was also confronted with much more complicated requirements than a socialist revolution would have faced in an advanced capitalist society. This beginning and the additional complex requirements imposed on the revolution left their mark on the entire process of socialist construction and created serious historical problems in its path. Each and every step in the historical development of socialism pursued in that country were devised and implemented in

---

[14] V.I. Lenin, *Collected Works*, Progress Publishers, Moscow, 1977, Volume 27, p. 131.

response to one or more of these complicated external as well as internal requirements imposed upon the system. Taking account of the impact of these external factors on the structures and internal functioning of socialism's historical models is especially important for the assessment not only of the relative share of the objective and subjective factors in the emergence of crisis in the socialist system but also of the role of the vanguard Party in the emergence of such crisis.

2. Building Socialism Under the Siege of Imperialism

The Bolsheviks' initial policy after taking power was not to immediately socialize the ownership of the means of production throughout society but to establish a form of state capitalism based on control of the key sectors of the economy, mixed management of private economic enterprises, and legal recognition of private ownership in agriculture, retail trade and small industries. Such an approach was in fact guided by the realities of Russian society. Their approach to the question of private property was cautious, particularly in relation to the industrial sector. To prevent the flight of capital and hence a sudden drop in production, they conceded to a coexistence, albeit fragile, between the public and private sectors. The revolutionary government nationalized only the key economic sectors, such as banking, grain procurement, transportation, oil and the military industry. The workers' committees in the private industries were limited to supervisory functions over the management; the right to make decisions and run the enterprise still resided with the private owners of the enterprises. Workers' committees were forbidden from violating the owners' rights or taking over the factory without government permission. In the agricultural sector, the Bolsheviks' first move after seizing power was to pass the land reform act of November 8, 1917, which confiscated the land of big landowners and distributed it among the peasants. This, too, meant an implicit recognition by the Bolsheviks of private property in agriculture.

But soon after the victory of the October Revolution, the Bolsheviks were faced with the invasion and occupation of Russian territory by 14 imperialist states and an imperialist-instigated civil war imposed on the country by the White Russians. Germany had occupied Ukraine. The White Russians had taken over the Urals, Siberia, the northern parts of Kazakhstan and other economically important areas. Poland was also occupying part of Russia. A point was reached where the Bolsheviks were in control of only 10 percent of the country's coal supplies, 25 percent of the iron foundries, less than 10 percent of the sugar beet production, and less than 50 percent of all grain production.[15] In such conditions, they had to fight for the survival of the revolutionary state in an unequal war against the occupying forces of 14 imperialist states as well as the White Russians. The Bolsheviks' first historical model, "War Communism," was developed and implemented in response to such conditions, with the goal of mobilizing all existing but limited economic resources of the country in defense of the socialist revolution and winning the imposed civil war.

The "War Communism" Model (1918-1921)

The "War Communism" model was based on the principle of state control over all economic and human resources of the country and the replacement of the market mechanism with an administrative distribution system. In light of the significance of agriculture in the country's economy, the first act within the framework of "War Communism" was

---

[15] Maurice Dobb, *Soviet Economic Development Since 1917*, International Publishers, New York, 1966, pp. 103-4.

to confiscate the excess production of the agricultural sector. The state police (*Cheka*) was dispatched to all villages to collect any excess production held by the wealthy and middle-income farmers.

Nationalization of the non-agricultural industries was another feature of "War Communism." This process, which began with the sugar industry in the spring of 1918, by the Fall of 1920 had taken over more than 37,000 units, of which more than half were small, non-mechanized units.[16] The 1920 Soviet industrial statistics show that over 5,000 of these nationalized units had only one employee.[17]

The third aspect of "War Communism" was the ban on all private trade. In 1918, private trade was completely banned and the state became the sole distributor of consumer goods. By the same token, the state established its control over the industrial workforce, limited the movement of industrial workers, and labor allocation was brought under administrative control. Heavy penalties were set for idleness and, on November 28, 1919, military discipline was imposed upon state employees. Money, as a means of exchange, lost its role and transactions between economic enterprises were handled through bookkeeping entries in accounting records. Differences in wages were almost abolished and the workers' wages were paid in goods. On the other hand, the state declared all city services and transportation free of charge.

Thus, from the very first step, the reality of civil war imposed itself upon the process of socialist construction in the form of "War Communism." Providing free services, equalizing wages, completely eradicating private ownership of the means of production in industry and of large land ownership in agriculture, eliminating the role of money in the economy, the state's full control over the allocation of society's material and human resources, complete state control

---

[16] Dobb, *op. cit.*, p. 106.

[17] Alec Nove, *An Economic History of the USSR*, Penguin, London, 1969, p. 70.

over the distribution of consumer goods, etc. — none of these were among policies prescribed by the theory of scientific socialism for the "first phase" of Communist society. Such form of organization of socialist society, which in many ways imitated the features of an advanced Communist society, was adopted only in response to the requirements of the period and for the sole purpose of achieving victory in the imposed civil war. This was not a model for socialist development, but one for the prevention of socialism's military defeat at the hands of the imperialist countries and the internal enemies of the working class.

"War Communism" was a tremendous political and military success in protecting the socialist state against its enemies. However, due to its incompatibility with the objective conditions of society, it had important negative consequences as well. Between 1918 and 1921, agricultural production plummeted. Wheat production plunged to one-half in Siberia and was cut to one-fourth in the Volga and Caucasus regions. This motivated many farmers to illegally hide part of their output from the state officials. In some areas, concealed quantities were as high as 20 percent of the total output.[18]

The link between the agricultural and the industrial sectors was also severed. The sharp drop in the farmers' purchasing power to the bare level of household survival took away their demand for the consumer goods produced in the industrial sector. The farmers' consumption level for the industrial goods fell to 12-15 percent of the pre-war level. All these factors angered the farmers who had hoped for relative prosperity after the land reforms. The farmers demanded abolition of state monopoly over the production and distribution of agricultural products.

On the other hand, lack of adequate material incentive for workers emanating from low incomes and a mechanical levelling of their wages caused problems for the industrial

---

[18] Dobb, *op. cit.*, p. 117.

sector as well. The level of industrial production dropped to 15 percent of the prewar period. An increasing number of workers were turning away from factories. Many of the people who had come to the urban areas in search of work left the cities. The urban population dropped from 2.6 million in 1917 to 1.2 million in 1920.[19] The labor shortage in the industrial sector was becoming more critical every day. By the end of 1920, strikes had become widespread. Finally, in March 1921, when the sailors of the "Kronstadt" naval base struck in support of the Petrograd workers, it became obvious that "War Communism," despite its tremendous success in achieving its political and military goals, was at the same time creating an ever deepening economic crisis for the country.

The economic side effects of "War Communism" clearly demonstrated the scientific accuracy of Marx's warnings about the dangers of "rushing ahead" in a socialist revolution. In his speech commemorating the fourth anniversary of the October Revolution, Lenin emphasized this fact:

> Borne along on the crest of the wave of enthusiasm, rousing first the political enthusiasm and then the military enthusiasm of the people, we expected to accomplish economic tasks just as great as political and military tasks we had accomplished by relying directly on this enthusiasm. We expected — or perhaps it would be truer to say that we presumed without having given it adequate consideration — to be able to organize the state production and the state distribution of products on communist lines in a small-peasant country directly as ordered by the proletarian state. Experience has proven that we were wrong. It appears that a number of transitional stages were necessary — state capitalism and socialism — in order to prepare by many years of effort — for the transition to communism. Not directly relying on enthusiasm, but aided by enthusiasm

---

[19] Nove, *op. cit.*, p. 94.

engendered by the great revolution, and on the basis of personal interest, personal incentive and business principles, we must first set to work in this small-peasant country to build solid gangways to socialism by way of state capitalism. Otherwise we shall never get to communism, we shall never bring scores of millions of people to communism. That is what experience, the objective course of the development of the revolution, has taught us.[20]

Nevertheless, it seems that this "rushing ahead" was more a consequence of objective factors imposed on the socialist revolution from outside than a result of subjectivism and lack of experience on the part of the Bolsheviks. As Lenin has himself emphasized: "War communism was thrust upon us by war and ruin. It was not, nor could it be, a policy that corresponded to the economic tasks of the proletariat. It was a temporary measure."[21] This "temporary measure," designed with the specific and limited aim of defending socialism against foreign aggression and war, achieved its political and military goals. Yet, its lack of correspondence to the "economic tasks of the proletariat" dictated that the model be abandoned immediately after it achieved its goals. And this is what actually happened.

The New Economic Policy (NEP) (1921-1928)

Just as "War Communism" was devised as a response against imperialist aggression and civil war, the NEP was formulated with the objective of relieving society of the economic crisis resulting from "War Communism." From the Bolsheviks' point of view, and Lenin himself, this "step backward" was a move towards coexistence with capitalism, and utilization of the profit for the purpose of reversing the

---

[20] *Collected Works*, Progress Publishers, Moscow, 1977, Volume 33, p. 58.

[21] Dobb, *op. cit.*, p. 123.

sharp decline in industrial and agricultural production.

From an economic point of view, NEP's most significant feature was the effort to mix socialism with a market economy. On this basis, the leadership of agricultural production was relegated to farmers themselves, and the management of the industrial sector, with the exception of heavy industries, transportation, banking and foreign trade, was mainly left to the private sector. State monopoly over trade and distribution was abolished and this function was once again relegated to the market. By 1923, close to 90 percent of the retail trade outlets, which handled over 75 percent of all retail trade, were privatized.[22]

The state's role was limited to providing "general guidance" for the economy through its control of basic industries and influencing economic trends through tax policies. Money, as a means of exchange, was again recognized. Monetary exchanges between state enterprises replaced exchanges effected through bookkeeping. In 1921, the State Bank reopened with the aim of "promoting economic growth." The bank removed all restrictions on private deposits, and the government announced that all private deposits with the State Bank would be immune from confiscation.

In the industrial sector, all economic enterprises with less than 20 employees were returned to the private sector; some were returned to their original owners and others leased to the emerging private entrepreneurs. Heavy industries, 98 percent of them state owned, also witnessed major changes. Except for energy, metal, military, transportation, banking and foreign trade, the rest were turned over to large "trusts" which enjoyed complete economic independence and, like their counterparts in the private sector, acted on the principle of profit maximization. With regard to their production, these "trusts" had no obligation towards the state, whose only link with these "trusts" was to collect taxes. The state

---

[22] *Ibid.*, p. 143.

would simply sign contracts with the "trusts" to buy their products. By 1923, 478 such "trusts" were established which together employed more than 75 percent of all workers in nationalized industries.[23] Even industries funded by the state were ordered to operate on the basis of profit and eliminate their need for state subsidies.

In agriculture, this privatization trend was put into practice at a much faster rate. In fact, the pillar of the NEP model was to win back the peasants, who made up the largest part of the country's labor force, and to guarantee their cooperation with the socialist state. The Bolsheviks used all their efforts to prevent a new rift between the peasants and the state. Consciously, and contrary to their real wishes, the Bolsheviks stayed away from all policies that might have angered the peasants. This was why the farmers were given a free hand in controlling their surplus production, while the state limited itself to levying a fixed tax rate on their "net surplus product." Peasants were allowed to sell their surplus products in the market, just as a private entrepreneur would, and to accumulate wealth from their profits. The state even permitted the farmers to lease their land and hire agricultural laborers.

This policy, while creating the necessary material incentives for increasing agricultural production, led to the growth of a layer of well-off farmers who became the source of serious problems for socialism later on in the course of its development. Despite the fact that Marx had referred to the affluent and semi-affluent farmers as die-hard enemies of socialism, the socialist state was forced by objective circumstances to forego its socialist plans and give serious economic concessions to affluent farmers in exchange for a rapid growth in agricultural output. These concessions went so far as outright subsidizing of the agricultural sector and artificially raising the prices of agricultural products at the expense of the industrial sector in 1923, when the imbalance between the

---

[23] *Ibid.*, p. 135.

two main economic sectors caused by "War Communism" had brought about a rise in the prices of industrial goods and a decline in the prices of agricultural products — a phenomenon known as the Scissors Crisis.[24]

Despite these retreats from socialist measures, the New Economic Plan was a big strategic success for the Bolsheviks. At the end of the "War Communism" era, the level of production in parts of industry and transportation had fallen to 20 percent of their prewar levels. The Communists managed, with the help of the NEP, to increase production to its previous level. The growth in agriculture was even more impressive. Here, in 1920, the production had fallen to 64 percent of its prewar level, but by 1928, it had risen to 118 percent of the 1920 level.[25] The government eliminated the budget deficit by 1923-4 and a year later achieved a positive balance in its budget. The value of the ruble stabilized, and was even being exchanged on the international currency markets. Thus, the NEP achieved its specified economic objectives.

Just as "War Communism" had reached its political and military objectives at the expense of economic production, the NEP guaranteed economic revival at the expense of certain political damages, especially as regards the process of socialist construction. In fact, the NEP as an economic model was not a socialist model based on planning but, as Lenin himself had stressed, a state capitalism model based on the profit motive. This model not only led to the emergence of layers of new capitalists in industry and affluent farmers in agriculture, but also subordinated the long-term goals of the socialist state to the exigencies of the market economy. This was

---

[24] For more information on the Scissors Crisis see Gregory and Stuart, *op. cit.,* pp. 57-60.

[25] G. W. Nutter, "The Soviet Economy: Retrospect and Prospect," in David Abshire and Richard V. Allen, *National Security: Political, Military and Economic Strategies in the Decades Ahead,* Praeger, New York, 1963, p. 165.

particularly apparent in heavy and basic industries. While only large state investments in production could guarantee the growth of socialism, the volume of capital stock in heavy industry was 23 percent less in 1924 than at its peak in 1917. In the same year, the total output of the steel industry, which constituted the main component of industrial equipment production, was reduced to only 23 percent of the 1913 level.[26] In 1926, almost eight years after the establishment of the Soviet State, the make-up of the country's industrial production was the same as that of 1912. While in 1912, 28 percent of the country's total manufacturing output was devoted to heavy industry, this share had grown to only 29 percent by 1926.[27] In other words, the country's industrial capacity had grown by a mere one percent, the existing equipment had grown old, and the framework of the NEP allowed for no strategic planning in the direction of advancing towards socialism.

Moreover, by 1926 the growth of industrial production had reached the limits of the existing capacity and had started to decline. As a result, the NEP could continue only on the basis of a one-sided growth of the agricultural sector — a policy which certainly contradicted the economic principles of socialist development. Thus the need for planned state investment in heavy industry was becoming increasingly clear. And this required a rapid accumulation of capital through bringing society's surplus product under state control. The NEP, after having achieved its specific objectives, had to be replaced by another model that could better serve the strategic goal of socialist economic development. This urgency was felt even more after the hope for proletarian revolution in the capitalist countries of Europe dissipated.

---

[26] Alexander Erlich, *The Soviet Industrialization Debate, 1924-1928*, Harvard University Press, Cambrige, 1960, pp. 105-106.

[27] Paul Gregory, *Socialist and Nonsocialist Industralization Patterns*, Praeger, New York, 1970, p. 28.

The "Rapid Industrialization" Model (1928-1945)

It was due to the realization of this urgency that between 1924 and 1928 serious discussions took place among the leaders of the Communist Party over the future model of socialist development.[28] Three distinct tendencies could be noticed within these debates. The speaker for the first tendency, I. A. Preobrazhenski, who belonged to the left wing of the Party, argued that the initial accumulation of capital for economic development should be achieved through a sharp reduction of consumption and the transfer of all of the agricultural sector's surplus product to the industrial sector. This model was based on the premise of the unbalanced development of the industry at the expense of agriculture in the short term. In the long run, however, after the initial phase of industrial development, material conditions would be created for the development of agriculture and the imbalances in the sectoral developments would thus be redressed. The principal assumption of this model was that the initial accumulation of capital would have to rely exclusively on the country's internal resources due to the impossibility of expanding trade with Western countries.[29]

On the opposite end of the spectrum was the model for unbalanced development of agriculture. Lev Shanin, who belonged to the right wing of the Party leadership, was the spokesman for this tendency. Basing his argument on the existing structure of the agricultural sector and the rural composition of the labor force, he proposed that initial capital investments should be made in agriculture since every ruble of investment in agriculture would yield higher returns as

---

[28] For a detailed description of the Soviet industrialization debate see Gregory and Stuart, *op. cit.*, pp. 66-94.

[29] Gregory and Stuart, *op. cit.*, pp. 70-74.

compared to industry and would thus guarantee a higher rate of economic development. Accordingly, the state would focus on increasing agricultural output, exporting this sector's surplus product and importing the machinery required by the industrial sector from abroad. Clearly, Shanin's model was based on the premise of expanding trade with advanced capitalist countries.[30]

Countering these two models was that of "balanced growth" proposed by N. I. Bukharin, the official spokesman of the right wing of the Party. He believed that both of these unbalanced development models, be it industrial or agricultural, would lead the economy into crisis again. He also argued that a rapid accumulation of capital combined with reduced consumption would culminate in "starvation" and would destroy the achievements of the "NEP." He thus insisted on a model based on a much slower rate of accumulation and growth that would preserve the balance between various sectors of the economy — between industry and agriculture, and between heavy and consumer goods industries. His model was based on the mechanism of an open market economy, promoting voluntary increase in production by farmers through raising the price of agricultural products, lowering the prices of industrial goods, and acquisition of industrial technology from abroad.[31]

What finally decided the outcome of this four-year debate was the deepening concern of the Party leadership with the growth of fascism in Europe and the increasing possibility of renewed military aggression by the imperialist countries. This issue manifested itself in various positions taken by the Party leadership, and especially by Stalin, on these different proposals. In the early stages of the debate, when the danger of foreign aggression was less real, the Party leadership leaned towards Bukharin's model and against that of the left wing.

---

[30] *Ibid.*, pp. 74-78.

[31] *Ibid.*, pp. 78-80.

However, as the danger grew, the need to industrialize the country with the help of its internal resources was increasingly felt. Bukharin's "balanced growth" model, which advocated a slower rate of growth and a heavy reliance on foreign trade, no longer fit this emergency situation. Finally, in 1928, the Party's Central Committee characterized the views of Bukharin and his followers as "right wing delusions" and declared its support for the "rapid industrialization" model. The importance of the external factors — i.e., the increased danger of imperialist aggression — in this decision is quite clear in the following passage from Stalin's speech in defense of the adoption of the "rapid industrialization" model for the Soviet Union:

> It is sometimes asked whether it is not possible to slow down the tempo a bit, to put a check on the movement. No, comrades, it is not possible! The tempo must not be reduced! On the contrary, we must increase it as much as it is within our powers and possibilities.... To slacken the tempo would mean falling behind. And those who fall behind get beaten. No, we refuse to be beaten! One feature of the history of old Russia was the continual beatings she suffered for falling behind. She was beaten by the Mongol Khans. She was beaten by the Turkish beys. She was beaten by the Swedish feudal lords. She was beaten by the Polish and Lithuanian gentry. She was beaten by British and French capitalists. She was beaten by the Japanese barons. All beat her — for her backwardness: for military backwardness, for cultural backwardness, for political backwardness, for industrial backwardness, for agricultural backwardness....
>
> This is why we must no longer lag behind....
>
> Do you want our socialist fatherland to be beaten and lose its independence? If you do not want this you must put an end to its backwardness in the shortest possible time.... There is no other way. This is why Lenin said during the October Revolution: "Either perish, or overtake and outstrip the advanced capitalist countries."
>
> We are fifty or a hundred years behind the advanced

countries. We must make good this distance in ten years. Either we do it, or they crush us.[32]

Reality proved Stalin's prediction. In 1941, less than a decade after this historic speech, Nazi Germany staged an all out military offensive against the Soviet Union with the purpose of its complete annihilation. And it was only through the speedy implementation of the "rapid industrialization" model that the Soviet Union managed to build the economic infrastructure necessary to defeat Hitler's military offensive, defend socialism, and spare the peoples of the rest of the world from the evil of fascism.

Naturally, after having taken such an important decision for a rapid industrialization of the country in order to "make good this distance in ten years," the Soviet state needed to adopt such economic measures that would make the achievement of this objective possible. Centralized economic planning was the only measure that could satisfy this need. In that situation, decentralized and indirect methods of economic management and control, and reliance on market mechanisms for achieving economic development — mechanisms which were very slow by nature — could not have been effective. Hence, the NEP had to be replaced by a centrally planned model. This was an objective, historical necessity caused not by the free will of the Soviet leadership but by the real and increasing danger of imperialist aggression from outside.

Thus, the leadership of the CPSU, which had earlier discarded Preobrazhenski's unbalanced industrial growth model, and the left wing along with it, wholeheartedly embraced his model and moved for its rapid implementation. The principles governing this model were exactly the same as those expounded by Preobrazhenski: sharp reduction in

---

[32] "The Tasks of the Business Executives," (Speech delivered at the First All-Union Conference of Managers of Socialist Industry, February 4, 1931), in J. Stalin, *Leninism: Selected Writings*, International Publishers, New York, 1942, pp. 199-200.

the social consumption level; total state control over production, distribution and prices of goods and services; complete transfer of surplus product from agriculture to the industrial sector; rapid capital accumulation in the industrial sector; emphasis on the growth of heavy industry as opposed to light and consumer industries; rapid transfer of the rural labor force from the farms to the cities and factories; a speedy literacy campaign and technical education of the labor force; and strict reliance on internal resources for economic development as opposed to reliance on foreign trade.

These principles were reflected in the Communist Party's five-year plans, the first of which was adopted in October 1928. According to the first five-year plan, the volume of fixed capital in heavy industry had to double within five years in order to prepare the ground for socialist development. For the first time, the socialist principle of "from each according to their ability, to each according to their contribution" was made the basis of all work. This principle was also used to facilitate the transfer of the workforce between different economic sectors as well as to encourage literacy and specialization. Unlike the "War Communism" model, which had imposed an institutional-military discipline upon the workforce, the "rapid industrialization" model functioned on the basis of voluntary work and increasing labor productivity through material incentives. The level of wages in agriculture, services and the public sector were intentionally reduced while workers' wages in heavy industry and other productive sectors were drastically increased. At the same time, the state provided free education in all schools and set up free on-the-job training for workers in all factories.

In the early 1930s, Stalin openly attacked "egalitarian tendencies among intellectuals" and rejected any effort in the direction of "identifying socialism with egalitarianism." In his address delivered at a conference of business executives, held on June 23, 1931, he said:

The cause [of heavy turnover of labor power] is the

wrong structure of wages, the "Leftist" practice of wage equalization.... In order to put an end to this evil we must abolish wage equalization and discard the old wage scales.... Marx and Lenin said that the difference between skilled labor and unskilled labor would exist even under socialism, even after classes had been abolished; that only under communism would this difference disappear and that, therefore, even under socialism "wages" must be paid according to work performed and not according to needs. But the equalitarians among our business executives and trade union officials do not agree with this and believe that under the Soviet system this difference has already disappeared. Who is right, Marx and Lenin, or the equalitarians? We must take it that it is Marx and Lenin who are right. But if that is so, it follows that whoever draws up wage scales on the "principle" of wage equalization, without taking into account the difference between skilled and unskilled labor, breaks with Marxism, breaks with Leninism....

But to get skilled workers we must give the unskilled worker a stimulus and prospect of advancement; of rising to a higher position. And the more boldly we do it the better.... To economize in this matter would be criminal, it would be going against the interests of our socialist industry.[33]

In line with these premises, the Party leadership introduced a planned system of wage differentiation as a fundamental principle of socialist construction. A system of wage differentiation based on the level of education, skill, job difficulty, and geographical location was established. The mechanism of wage differentiation was used as an effective material incentive for workers in their choice of work as well as in increasing their skills. By 1934, the average wage difference between skilled and unskilled workers had reached the ratio of 4 to 1, and by 1956, before the opposite trend started, it

---

[33] *Ibid.*, pp. 206-207.

reached the ratio of 8 to 1.[34] In certain instances, in 1934, while some skilled workers in heavy industry received monthly wages of 1,420 rubles, wages for the unskilled workers in non-manufacturing sectors did not exceed 50 rubles a month — a ratio of 28.3 to 1.[35] This method of labor allocation and of increasing labor productivity constituted the cornerstone of the "rapid industrialization" model throughout the period of its implementation.

The achievements of the "rapid industrialization" model, within the framework of its predefined objectives, were impressive and historically unprecedented. Between 1928 and 1940, industrial production grew at an average annual rate of 11 percent.[36] Gross industrial capital stock grew from 34.8 billion rubles in 1928 to 75.7 billion rubles in 1933, 119 billion rubles in 1937 and 170 billion rubles in 1940.[37] The share of agriculture in gross national product (GNP) was reduced from 49 percent in 1928 to 29 percent in 1940, while the share of the industrial sector grew from 28 percent to 45 percent in the same period.[38] Between 1928 and 1937, the share of heavy manufacturing in the country's total manufacturing output grew from 31 percent to 63 percent, while output per worker in heavy industry grew from 94 percent of the light industries in 1928 to 140 percent in 1933.[39]

Changes in the labor force were also amazing. The share of full-time workers in the country's total labor force grew from 57 percent in 1928 to 70 percent in 1937. The share of industrial workers in the total work force grew at an average

---

[34] Gregory and Stuart, *op. cit.*, pp. 197-198.

[35] A. Bergson, *The Structure of the Soviet Wages, Harvard University Press*, Cambridge 1944, p. 127.

[36] Gregory and Stuart, *op. cit.*, p. 82.

[37] *Ibid.*

[38] *Ibid.*

[39] *Ibid.*

annual rate of 8.7 percent, increasing from 18 percent of total work force in 1928 to 29 percent in 1940.[40] Women increasingly entered the work force. By 1939, 71 percent of all women between the ages of 16 and 59 were members of the labor force.[41] By the same year, the illiteracy rate had declined from 56 percent (1928) to 20 percent; and by 1940, more than 14 million people had more than a seventh-grade education and more than one million had finished high school.[42] The number of graduates from specialized secondary institutions grew rapidly from 1.3 million in 1926 to 7.9 million in the late 1950s.[43] During the same period, the number of full-time university students increased by more than 800 percent. According to a state decree, 75 percent of students admitted to high schools and technical colleges had to be from working-class or peasant families.

The share of the socialist sector in the economy rose sharply. Between 1928 and 1937, this sector's share rose from 65.7 percent to 99.6 percent of the country's total capital stock; from 82.4 percent to 99.8 percent of gross industrial production; and from 3.3 percent to 98.5 percent of gross agricultural production.[44] Alongside this trend, education, health services and social insurance were declared free, and from 1936 onwards state subsidies were given to single mothers and to mothers with many children. The growth of the socialist sector also coincided with the rise in the share of free social services (Communist consumption) in the workers' total income. Free social services, growing at an annual rate of 15.7 percent, had doubled between 1928 and 1940, making up 10 percent of the gross national prod-

---

[40] *Ibid.*

[41] *Ibid.*, p. 206.

[42] *Ibid.*, p. 208.

[43] *Ibid.*, p. 209.

[44] *Ibid.*, p. 83.

uct.[45] As a result, the share of free social services in the workers' total income grew from a low of 28 percent in 1927, to 34.5 percent in 1935 and to more than 38 percent in 1944. By 1944, every worker in the Soviet Union was receiving, in addition to his/her own wages, an amount close to 40 percent of these wages from the national (communist) consumption fund free of charge.[46] And this was at the time when the state was consciously planning to limit social consumption.

Naturally, achieving these tremendous objectives within such a short period of time could not have come about without some sacrifices. Some of these were consciously planned and built into the "rapid industrialization" model itself. For example, the average annual growth in agricultural production between 1928 and 1940 was only one percent, and the labor force employed in this sector was dropping by an average rate of 2.5 percent annually, reducing the share of agriculture in the total labor force from 71 percent in 1928 to 51 percent in 1940.[47] This was the direct result of the wage differential policy aimed at voluntary transfer of the labor force from rural areas to the industrial centers. Nevertheless, labor productivity in agricultural grew by 17 percent during the same period.[48] Moreover, in order to limit social consumption, the state sharply raised the prices of consumer goods with the exception of basic necessities. Between 1928 and 1937, the consumer and agricultural goods prices were increased by 700 percent and 539 percent respectively. As a result, the share of household consumption in the gross national product dropped from 80 percent in 1928 to 53 percent

---

[45] *Ibid.*

[46] Janet Chapman, *Real Wages in Soviet Russia Since 1928*, Harvard University Press, Cambridge, 1963; Table 20: "Soviet Statements on Benefits as a Contribution to Wages," p. 140.

[47] Gregory and Stuart, *op. cit.*, p. 83.

[48] *Ibid.*

in 1937, and then to 49 percent in 1940.[49]

On the other hand, central planning for the production and distribution of thousands of socially produced commodities in a country covering one-sixth of the surface of the earth was not an easy task. The First Five-Year Plan mapped out the output quantity and the distribution patterns for approximately 900 commodities to be produced by the socialist sector of the economy. This number increased in the following five-year plans to 3,000 and then to 10,000, 30,000 and 200,000 in the subsequent plans. Obviously, such extensive planning of production and distribution required a tremendous amount of computing power. According to one research,

> [T]he number of interrelationships among objects of economic planning grows in proportion to the square of the number of objects themselves. For example, in drawing the plan for the Soviet machine-building industry, which turns out 125 thousand types of commodities, the planner must take account of over 15 billion (or, 125,000 x 125,000) relations among these various products.... Nor is this the end ... a single commodity produced in a hundred establishments is likely to involve more calculations and decisions than a hundred commodities in one.... For example, a modern radio-spectrometer, a relatively simple device, consists of 264 components produced by 150 separate factories.... No wonder Soviet planners are said to be drowning in 'a paper ocean.'"[50]

By the mid-1930s, this problem increasingly manifested itself in shortages or excess production due to computing errors, raising the issue of the need for decentralization of

---

[49] *Ibid*

[50] For a detailed description of the growing complexity of socialist central planning in the Soviet Union and various proposals for decentralization of economic planning during the 1930s, see, e.g.: Leon Smolinski and Peter Wiles, "The Soviet Planning Pendulum," in George R. Feivel, ed., *New Currents in Soviet Type Economies*, International Textbook Company, Scranton, Pennsylvania, 1969, pp. 296-315.

economic planning to the level of the republics. However, despite the recognition of the need for decentralization by the Soviet leadership, the threat of imperialist aggression and the negative effects of decentralization on the country's military preparedness blocked such reforms.

Nevertheless, with the continuous growth of socialism the need for advanced computing technology was increasingly felt to the point of becoming a strategic necessity. Not only the Soviet Union, but no other country could have tackled this issue alone. But the imperialist countries, recognizing socialism's critical need for advanced computing technology, imposed a strict international ban on transfer of all forms of computer technology to the Soviet Union and turned this policy into an central and strategic element of their economic blockade against the USSR. Up until the time of the dismantling of the Soviet state in 1992, all imperialist countries fiercely and assiduously followed this strategic policy, which played a crucial role in disrupting the socialist economic planning in the USSR during the past several decades.

The problems, however, were not economic alone. Collectivizing agricultural production and expanding public ownership in that sector from 3.3 percent to 98.5 percent in less than a decade met with a stiff challenge from the well-off farmers who had greatly prospered during the NEP period. From the socialist state's point of view, the key to the success of the "rapid industrialization" model was state control over the surplus product in agriculture, and the resistance put forth by wealthy farmers could easily cause the defeat of the whole model. That is why the state took up the policy of forced collectivization and moved rapidly and decisively to suppress all opposition to this project. The excesses committed by the socialist state in implementing this policy had deep and serious negative ramifications for the unity workers and peasants, creating both political and popular difficulties for the state. The true historical dimensions and the methods used in this suppression have long been a subject of serious debate, and judgment in this matter requires closer historical investigation. Yet, it is quite clear that the collectivization of agricultural production constituted an integral component of the "rapid industrialization" model, and its side-effects must therefore be analyzed within the framework of the objectives set for the model as a whole.

Moreover, in an attempt to silence all opposition to the "rapid industrialization" of the country, a similar process was initiated within the Communist Party itself. Any form of opposition was construed as an effort to diminish the country's readiness to face an immanent imperialist aggression. Many of the Communist Party's distinguished leaders, who played key roles in the victory of the October Revolution, were charged with treason and espionage for imperialism, and were sentenced to death or imprisonment. Although many of these leaders were later rehabilitated, these repressions left a lasting mark on the Party and paved the way for the subsequent development of many negative tendencies within the Party.

One may, however, dare to say that the most important and enduring side effect of the "rapid industrialization" model was to obscure and confound the logical and historical boundaries between the structures and responsibilities of the Communist Party and those of the socialist state. The need to guide in practice the process of rapid industrialization of the country forced the Communists to assume the executive responsibilities of the state, even at the lowest levels, and to become the caretakers of the state affairs on a daily basis. This had serious effects on the Party's role as well as on its internal structures, and became decisive in forming the Party's policies in the following periods of socialist construction in the Soviet Union. The continuance into the following periods of this permutation of structures and responsibilities of the Party and the state, although largely unavoidable from an objective and historical point of view during the period of rapid industrialization, became one of the most important causes of crisis in socialism later on. The subjective factors of the crisis are discussed in Part III.

3. The Destructive Effects of Fascist Aggression

Fascist Germany's military aggression against the Soviet Union and the occupation of part of the land, which took place with the instigation and implicit agreement of other imperialist powers, destroyed a large part of the socialist advances achieved during the 1930s. More than 20 million people of the Soviet Union, a large part of the country's labor force and its most revolutionary citizens, perished in the war against fascism. The occupying German forces pillaged 1,710 cities and towns in the most industrialized area of the country, and burned down more than 70,000 rural towns; 32,000 industrial units and 65,000 kilometers of railroad tracks were ruined; 98,000 cooperatives and nearly 5,000 state agricultural enterprises, tractor and farm machinery stations were looted. Tens of thousands of hospitals, schools, art schools, higher education institutes and libraries were completely destroyed. In total, the damage from the fascist invasion of the Soviet Union was more than 2.6 trillion rubles, 680 billion rubles of which were material values.[51]

No country in any war in human history ever endured so many casualties and so much damage. Heavy damage was previously inflicted on the Soviet Union during the civil war and it took more than six years, from 1921 to 1928 to recover. However, the destruction from the fascist invasion could not be compared to anything else. With the devastation of the country's industrial and agricultural infrastructure,

---

[51] *History of the Communist Party of the Soviet Union*, Foreign Languages Publishing House, Moscow, 1960, p. 614.

even the limited consumption facilities that existed had dissipated. People were facing severe difficulties in satisfying their basic needs — food, clothing, shoes, shelter, health, fuel, etc. The principle of socialist distribution was disrupted and the state was forced to reinstate the rationing mechanism of the War Communism era. The Party, the state and the heroic peoples of the Soviet Union had to begin anew the difficult road once travelled. And, once again, they had to travel the road without any outside help and with sole reliance on their own limited internal resources. The process of socialist construction was set back for more than ten years and had to start all over again from where it was at the beginning of the "rapid industrialization" model ten years earlier.

The socialist system, which had demonstrated its tremendous strength during the war, proved its constructive might once again. The fourth five-year plan reached its goals in four years and three months. Within two and a half years, the country's industries were revived. More than 6,000 large industrial units, equivalent to the first and second five-year plans combined, were rebuilt and started operations again. By 1948, the volume of industrial output surpassed that of the pre-war period, and by 1950, exceeded the pre-war level by 73 percent. By the same year, labor productivity in industry was 37 percent higher than its 1940 level.[52]

Rebuilding in agriculture was even more difficult, especially because of the drought of 1946. After the war, in 1945, the country's cultivated land area was 25 percent less than in 1940. Government stockpiles of grain, cotton and meat had dwindled to one half and of milk to one third of the amounts available in the year before the war. Due to war casualties, far fewer able bodied workers were available to work on farms, especially since a large of part of the rural work force was enticed to the cities for rebuilding the industries. Nevertheless, the tractor factories were rapidly rebuilt

---

[52] *Ibid.*, p. 675.

and, by 1950, agricultural production reached its pre-war levels with the help of a smaller work force but better material and technical support.[53]

Thus, relying on the "rapid industrialization" model, the Soviet Union succeeded in reconstructing its industrial and agricultural infrastructure and repair the war damages by the middle of 1950s. The Communist Party and the Soviet state, under the most difficult conditions, had transformed the USSR into an advanced industrial country within a short period of time. Over a period of less than three decades, between 1928-56, the country's industrial production had grown at an average annual rate of 12.7 percent and had reached a level 770 percent greater than in 1928; the gross national product had grown at an annual rate of more than 15 percent (10 percent according to some Western studies); illiteracy was eliminated; free health care and education were provided for everyone; and even by the admission of Western economists, consumer goods production had grown at an annual average rate of 5.8 percent despite the state's planned efforts to limit social consumption.[54] But in spite of all these achievements, the destruction resulting from the fascist invasion undeniably delayed the process of socialist construction in the Soviet Union for more than a decade. This ten-year delay had weakened the relative position of the Soviet Union *vis-a-vis* the advanced capitalist countries, especially against the emerging power of U.S. imperialism, which had suffered minimal damage during the course of the war.

The heroic victory of the Soviet Union in the war against fascism and socialism's impressive success in rebuilding the war damages in a short period of time created a great deal of moral respect and authority for the Communist Party and the Soviet state among the working class and the people

---

[53] *Ibid.,* pp. 677-678.

[54] Gregory Grossman, "Thirty Years of Soviet Industrialization," in George R. Feiwel, *op. cit.,* pp. 43-44.

of the USSR as well as the peoples of the world. Despite all remaining problems, the support of the people and of the working class of the Soviet Union for the Communist Party and the socialist state had reached unprecedented levels. This moral authority and respect, more than any other factor, caused a great deal of fear among imperialist powers who had focused their efforts on defeating socialism for the past several decades.

4. Cold War and the Arms Race

The explosion of atomic bombs over Hiroshima and Nagasaki by U.S. imperialism and the annihilation of hundreds of thousands of innocent lives was less a means of forcing Japanese imperialism into military surrender than it was a military warning to the Soviet Union and a signal for the beginning of the Cold War against socialism. During the war, while the Soviet Union was facing the destruction of its material and human resources, U.S. imperialism, across the ocean and away from the direct impact of the war, was busy arming itself with nuclear weapons. The military disparity resulting from the development of nuclear weapons by the United States was used by the U.S. and other imperialist powers as a means to bring the weakened socialist state to its knees. To this end, they even employed, rather than punished and imprisoned, many of the German nuclear weapons experts who had a hand in the annihilation of millions of people by the fascist regime.

Imposition of the Cold War by the imperialist governments, especially the United States, with the aim of destroying the socialist state turned into a long, drawn out and disastrous arms race for socialism. The need to confront imperialism's nuclear threat forced the Soviet Union into a program of massive arms build-up which absorbed a large portion of its badly needed resources. For capitalism, arms production was a natural source of capital accumulation and super profits for the ruling class. But for socialism, arms production was a damaging and destructive endeavor that would only gobble up the resources needed for socialist construction, acting as a huge drain on society's Communist consumption fund.

As a result of the arms race, investments in modern technology were primarily shifted to military industries, hindering technological development in the civilian sector of the economy. This phenomenon, in turn, limited the growth of non-military production and limited the system's ability to improve the working people's standard of living, thus reducing socialism's attractiveness *vis-a-vis* capitalism.

This situation, imposed on socialism from outside, turned into an effective anti-socialist propaganda tool in the hands of imperialist powers. Capitalism's ideological campaign against socialism took a new and increasingly complex form. The peoples of the Soviet Union and other socialist countries were constantly bombarded by anti-socialist and pro-capitalist propaganda through "Radio Free Europe" and other similar media, such as television, satellites, newspapers and magazines, and even Western tourists, among whom were plenty of paid agents and provocateurs. Capitalist propaganda was directly questioning the credibility of such concepts as public ownership and international working-class solidarity as well as the level of social welfare in socialist countries. At the same time, the imperialist powers were using all their efforts to directly sabotage and create havoc in the socialist countries, from the Soviet Union to China, the German Democratic Republic and Cuba.

Imperialism's cold-war propaganda and military campaign against socialism was part of a carefully planned and internationally financed aggression plan which the socialist governments could not effectively counter with their limited resources. In this regard, one may just take note of the fact that despite its massive economic growth, the Soviet Union's gross national product in 1971 was only 55 percent of that of the United States. Only after the downfall of the socialist states in the Soviet Union and other Eastern European countries was it revealed that during the Cold War, the United States government alone had hired tens of thousands of agents and was spending more than $15 billion annually for espionage and other destructive acts against the Soviet Union.[55]

The heavy expenditure imposed by the Cold War and the arms race had serious negative effects on the development of socialism. The growth rate of the Soviet economy was reduced in comparison with the pre-war era. The annual growth rate dropped from an average of 15 percent in the 1940s, to 10 percent in the 1950s and 6.7 percent between 1960 and 1972. The growth rate of the Soviet economy had still averaged about 8.3 percent annually between 1950 and 1972, which was more than double that of the United States during the same period.[56] However, given the qualitative difference between the two economic systems — especially the great responsibility of the socialist state to provide for the basic needs of all its citizens (a responsibility that does not exist for the capitalist state), and the historical task of guaranteeing an uninterrupted growth of the Communist sector of the economy — such a continuous drop in the economic growth rate could only mean trouble for the socialist system.

As a result, a slowdown in economic growth, combined with imperialism's anti-socialist propaganda campaign and its incessant sabotages, created the material ground for the deepening of the crisis and its elevation to the political level. But the existence of objective factors alone could not in itself mean the end of the road and the defeat of socialist rule. The Communist Party and the socialist state, at different

---

[55] Victor Perlo, "The Economic and Political Crisis in the USSR," *Political Affairs*, August 1991, p. 12.

[56] Gregory and Stuart, *op. cit.*, Table 25: "Long-term Growth of GNP in the USSR and USA," p. 378.

stages and under much harsher conditions — military occupation, social backwardness, drop in the level of production,
fascist aggression, etc. — had overcome the crises by adopting
appropriate measures and adequate socioeconomic models.
What caused the crisis to reach a political level this time was
the subjective errors made by the Party and the socialist
state in dealing with these objective, external factors and
their deviations from the fundamental theoretical principles
of scientific socialism in their efforts to devise new socialist
models adequate for the advancement of society towards
Communism.

Part Three:

The Subjective/Internal Factors Contributing to the Crisis of Socialism

The impressive achievements of socialism over three decades, under the most difficult and unfavorable objective-historical and international conditions, not only demonstrated socialism's immense capability to advance human society on the world scale, but also illustrated the important and critical role of the Communist Party in charting the road towards Communism. Socialism's victory over backwardness and fascism, and the addition of eleven other countries to the socialist camp after World War II, not only did not reduce the responsibilities of the Communist Party and the Soviet state but added new sets of internal and international responsibilities to the difficult task of building socialism under the siege of capitalism. From then on, the Soviet Union was faced with responsibility of providing economic and political assistance to the new socialist countries in addition to its original task of guaranteeing the development of socialism within its own borders. This put a much heavier economic burden on the USSR and necessitated a further increase in both the quantity and quality of economic production, additional improvements in labor productivity, and a drastic increase in the social wealth of the country.

At the same time, the unbalanced model of "rapid industrialization," despite all its tremendous achievements, had specific negative economic and political consequences, the continuation of which could seriously damage the process of socialist construction. In fact, some of these negative consequences had already left their marks, thus necessitating fundamental changes in the existing model of socialist development.

From the economic point of view, the agricultural sector was in a dire situation. Agricultural production during this period had grown by an annual average of only one percent. Peasants, especially in the cooperatives, had a poor standard of living. In 1950, their average income was less than 10 percent of those of the workers in the state farms and 5 percent of those of the urban industrial workers.[57] A significant gap had arisen between the standards of living of the rural and urban workers. Agricultural production was not enough to satisfy the growing demand of the city dwellers.

On the other hand, the long term focus on heavy industry and the lack of growth of light and consumer industries had brought about a shortage of consumer goods. This was in fact increasingly affecting production, especially in the heavy industries. The high wages paid to workers in heavy industry had drastically raised their purchasing power, but the lack of consumer goods had made spending of this higher income impossible. The incentive for more and better work in search of higher income had lost its meaning for the workers, thus negatively affecting labor productivity in the industrial sector. Also, the one-sided emphasis on quantitative increase in the volume of industrial output over several decades, even though out of necessity, had left a negative impact on the quality of commodities. Consequently, improving the quality of goods had become one of the essential requirement of the time.

---

[57] G. E. Shroeder and B. S. Severin, "Soviet Consumption and Income Policies in Perspective," in *Soviet Economy in a New Perspective: A Compendium of Papers Submitted to the Joint Economic Committee, Congress of the United States,* October 14, 1976, p. 629.

Moreover, rapid economic growth had created a more diverse and complex infrastructure for the socialist economy, making its management much more difficult. Up to this point, industrial growth had basically relied on increasing production through quantitative growth of investment and the transfer of the labor force from the rural areas to the cities. However, the need for increasing the rate of return on investments and improving the productivity of the existing labor force had become ever more critical. Together, all these factors required the adoption of new types of planning and economic management methods.

The "rapid industrialization" model had certain negative political consequences as well, the elimination of which had become critical for the further development of socialism. The forced collectivization of agriculture and the suppressions that followed this policy, along with the depressed level of agricultural wages for a long period of time, had seriously damaged the unity between workers and peasants. In addition, administrative methods used for planning production had given rise to bureaucracy and had facilitated the emergence of a growing technocratic layer within the state itself. Even more critical, this process had engulfed the Communist Party in the bureaucratic processes of the state. Socialist democracy had become limited to a great extent and the level of mass participation in the decision making processes was thereby reduced.

Democracy within the Party was impaired due to many objective reasons, especially the war. The Party Congress was not convened for over thirteen years (from 1939 to 1952), and individual leadership had on the whole replaced collective leadership. Most importantly, the lines of demarcation between the structures and responsibilities of the Communist Party and those of the socialist state had faded and signs of bureaucratic corruption and abuse of power and position among Communists in charge of the state apparatus had become ever more noticeable.

These factors, as well as many others, necessitated fundamental changes in socialism's socioeconomic model as well as in the methods of leadership of society. The Communist Party in its 20th Congress, which was held in February 1956, almost four years after the death of Joseph Stalin, addressed these issues. But, unfortunately, the solutions proposed and models adopted by the 20th Congress, rather than resolving the past problems, became new breeding ground for more serious problems which eventually culminated in a crisis for socialism. It was the first time that the Party, not by the force of objective/external factors residing beyond its control, but by its own volition and out of its own subjective errors, adopted certain policies that added to the difficulties of the process of socialist construction in the Soviet Union.

1. The "Rapid Consumption Growth" Model and the Grounds for Economic Crisis

The Communist Party's 20th Congress correctly placed the resolution of the economic and political problems resulting from the "rapid industrialization" model at the top of its agenda. Even before the Congress, the Party leadership had spoken of having "laid bare serious shortcomings in the Party, State and economic activities" during the Central Committee's July 1953 Plenum. It had attributed this "major irregularity" to "the violation of Leninist standards of Party life and the principles of Bolshevik leadership, as a consequence of the personality cult," as well as a lack of "collective leadership, or proper criticism and self-criticism, in the activity of the Central Committee and its Political Bureau." The same Plenum of the Central Committee had also noted that there had been "gross violations of Socialist legality" by some "adventurers" aimed at weakening "the Party and its leadership" and the "Government of the U.S.S.R.," and had taken appropriate decisions to correct the situation. Also, in its September 1953, June 1954 and January 1955 Plenums, the Central Committee had "critically appraised" the "state of agriculture" and had attributed the "lagging" of the rural economy to "both objective and subjective reasons, including to "inefficient leadership," "undue centralization of planning" and "violations of the Leninist principle of giving the collective farmers material incentive to increase agricultural output." The Central Committee's July 1955 Plenum had also emphasized the need for ensuring "a further powerful expansion of industry through better organization of production and the introduction of the latest achievements of science and technology." It declared that "technical progress in industry" was "an important means of speeding up the country's economic development, raising labor productivity and providing a material and technical basis for Communism."[58]

The 20th Congress, however, approached the negative political phenomena in a superficial and formal manner. It attributed all such phenomena — the breakdown of collective leadership and other aspects of the principle of democratic centralism, growth of bureaucracy in state organs, careerism, abuse of power and position by the Party cadre and leaders, and violations of the principles of socialist democracy throughout society — merely to Stalin's "personality cult." No attempt was made to find the structural roots of these phenomena, especially with regard to the fading of the lines of demarcation between state and Party organs or the growth of bureaucratic tendencies within the Party itself. Although resolutions were passed on "overcoming the personality cult and its consequences" in order to guarantee that "phenomena of this kind would never again arise in the Party and the country,"[59] a lack of a fundamental approach to the structural

---

[58] *History of the Communist Party of the Soviet Union*, Foreign Languages Publishing House, Moscow, 1960, pp. 653-663.

[59] *Ibid.*, p. 670.

roots of these problems kept the Party from arriving at a principled resolution of the problems. As later developments showed, this half-hearted attempt actually left the doors open for further growth of the these negative phenomena in both the Party and the state. Ascribing all these negative phenomena to "Stalin's personality cult" also provided the enemies of socialism with a golden opportunity to carry out their anti-Communist campaigns under the guise of personal attacks on Stalin.

More decisive than this, however, was the economic model adopted mainly (but not fully) in accordance with the guidelines of the 20th Congress. The 20th Congress gave the following general framework for the sixth five-year national economic development plan of the USSR for the period of 1956-60:

> — to continue to give priority to the development of heavy industry — ferrous and non-ferrous metallurgy, the oil, coal, chemical and engineering industries;
>
> — consistently to put into practice Lenin's behests regarding the country's electrification... and improve in every way the building industry so that it might meet all the requirements of capital construction in industry, of housing construction and the building of cultural and other amenities...;
>
> — to make the most effective use of the country's rich natural resources, to tap new sources of raw materials, fuel and electric power...;
>
> — to work persistently to accelerate technical progress: by introducing in industry the latest achievements of science and technology...;
>
> — to perfect the organization of production through greater specialization and coordination of factories;
>
> — to speed up the rate of production of consumer goods...;
>
> — to continue unremittingly to advance agriculture, to complete the comprehensive mechanization of the whole of agricultural production within the shortest possible time...;
>
> — to achieve a further rise in the people's living standards:

to increase the real wages of industrial, professional and office workers, primarily of the low-paid groups, to increase the incomes of collective farmers, gradually to shorten the working day of industrial, professional and office workers without reducing wages, to increase pensions, and to carry out other improvements in the social services;

— to encourage in every way the creative effort and initiative of the people in increasing labor productivity...;

— systematically to improve the work of local government institutions and trade union and Komsomol organizations, and to enhance their role in the country's economic life.[60]

The framework adopted by the sixth five-year plan included all the requirements of socialist development at that particular stage: continued emphasis on the expansion of heavy industry through the use of modern technology and improvements in labor productivity; increased returns on investments through advancing technology and labor productivity; closer attention to the consumption needs of the working people; elevation of the peasants' standard of living; modernization of agriculture and increasing agricultural output; and increasing the role of trade unions and councils in the decision making process. These principles inspired the formulation of a "rapid consumption growth" model which, while achieving important milestones in this direction, was ultimately derailed as a result of certain incorrect policies.

The first step in the "rapid consumption growth" model was a sharp increase in the level of wages, especially in the agricultural sector. The minimum monthly wage was increased across the whole economy from 27-35 rubles in 1957, to 40-45 rubles in 1962[61] and then to 60-70 rubles in 1968.[62]

---

[60] *Ibid.*, pp. 668-669.

[61] Murray Yanowitch, "The Soviet Income Revolution," *Slavic Review,* Vo. 22, No. 4, December 1963, pp. 663-695.

[62] Emily Clark Brown, "Continuity and Change in the Soviet Labor Market," in M. Bornstein and D. F. Fusfeld, eds., *The Soviet Economy: A Book of Reading,*

Following the plan guidelines, the level of agricultural wages was raised aggressively. The average annual wages in this sector rose from 89 rubles per year in 1950 to 330 rubles per year by 1960, and to 614 rubles per year (almost seven times) by 1965.[63] The corresponding numbers for non-agricultural workers rose from 830 rubles in 1950 to 1,008 rubles in 1960 and to 1,190 rubles (around 1.5 times) in 1965.[64] Even more impressive was the rise in the annual wages of the peasants on the collective farms: from 43 rubles in 1950 to 221 rubles in 1960 and 483 rubles (more than 11 fold) in 1965. On the state farms, the annual wages were increased from 459 rubles in 1950 to 559 rubles in 1960 and 900 rubles (almost doubled) by 1965.[65] Thus, between 1950 and 1965, the average annual agricultural wages increased from 11 percent to 52 percent of those in the non-agricultural sector. This rapid rise in wages continued in the following years as well.

Unfortunately, such rapid and extensive wage increases were not accompanied by a similar growth in the production of consumer goods. Despite the several-fold increase in wages, until 1965 the growth in per capita production of the light and consumer goods industries was, for instance, only 145 percent in the food industry and 123 percent in the household goods industry. The only significant increase in production was in the durable goods industry (such as refrigerators, televisions, washing machines, etc.), which grew by 800 percent between 1950 and 1965. But even this increase could not meet the working people's growing demand which had been held back for several decades. For example, in 1965, on average, 22 radios, 16 television sets, 7 refrigerators, 3.5 vacuum cleaners, 3.5 sewing machines and 8 furniture sets

---

Homewood, Illinois, Richard D. Irwin Inc., 4th ed., 1974, p. 176.

[63] Shroeder and Severin, *op. cit.*, p. 629.

[64] *Ibid.*

[65] *Ibid.*

were produced per 1,000 population.[66] In 1968, while there were 540 telephones per every 1,000 population in the United States, there were only 45 telephones per every 1,000 population in the Soviet Union (a ratio of 12 to one).[67]

On the other hand, while the "rapid consumption growth" model followed the western consumption patterns in emphasizing the growth of household consumption, the share of workers' social consumption (i.e., their share of income from the Communist consumption fund), which had reached 38 percent by 1944, actually dropped to 35 percent during 1950-56 — a figure that was even lower than that of 1935.[68] Even though consumption had increased in absolute terms during 1955-65, the rise could not compare to the quicker pace of wage increases. For example, between 1955 and 1965, the per capita housing space grew by only 42 percent, from 4.8 to 6.8 square meters, barely more than the 1928 figure of 5.8.[69] In 1968, nearly 30 percent of urban houses were still without running water. In 1969, 20 percent of the dwellings in the Russian Republic were still without running water and sewage, 25 percent without central heating and 40 percent without a shower or bath.[70] Thus, the rise in the level of social comfort and standard of living did not match the rise in the level of wages. While the annual growth rate of per capita consumption was more than 6 percent during 1950-55, it was reduced to 3.5 percent in 1956-60 and 2.7 percent in 1961-65.[71]

The rapid increase in cash incomes over a short period of

---

[66] Gertrude E. Shroeder, "Consumption in the USSR: A Survey," in Bornstein and Fusfeld, *op. cit.*, pp. 302-303.

[67] *Ibid.*, p. 304.

[68] Janet Chapman, *op. cit.*, p. 140.

[69] Gertrude E. Shroeder, *op. cit.*, p. 303.

[70] *Ibid.*, pp. 279-281.

[71] *Ibid.*, p. 276.

time, without a corresponding rise in the production of consumer goods, led to an annual growth rate of 20 percent in workers' idle savings between 1965 and 1968. While in 1960, the average savings of a worker was around 10 rubles, this per capita savings increased to almost 350 rubles (equal to four months' wages of an urban worker) by 1968. In 1969, 70 percent of the wage earners' additional income was being deposited in savings accounts. In large measure, this was due to lack of consumer goods.[72] This trend not only sapped workers' material incentive for more and better work but also encouraged a black market for existing goods as well. It created an underground economy based on corruption and bribery among government bureaucrats, especially those responsible for the distribution of consumer goods in society. Income from unproductive activities grew rapidly. This lead to the formation and growth of certain parasitic layers in society and within the state organs. The socialist principle of "income in exchange for productive social labor" was increasingly violated by these parasitic layers who lived off bribery and extortion of the working class. This was the starting point of the process of estrangement of the masses from the state and hence from the Communist Party as the leading Party of socialist society.

More damaging than this, however, was the policy of mechanical levelling of wages across the whole economy. Immediately after the 20th Congress, steps were taken towards eliminating the wage differentials. Within only three years, between 1956 and 1959, half of the socialist wage differentials established over the past 22 years were eliminated. By 1966, more than 87 percent of the Soviet labor force had a monthly income of between 40 and 160 rubles (60 percent between 40 and 100 rubles), and the number of those with an income of higher than 200 rubles per month did not exceed 2.5 percent of the total labor force. In contrast, in

[72] *Ibid.*, p. 288.

1934, only 52 percent of the Soviet labor force had a monthly income of between 40 and 160 rubles and the number of those earning more that 200 rubles a month exceeded 18 percent of the total labor force. (In 1934, 1.3 percent, and in 1966, only one percent of the working people had a monthly income of less than 40 rubles.) In industry, the differential between the wages of skilled and unskilled workers were dramatically reduced. By 1960, the difference between the maximum and the minimum wages based on skill, which was more than 4 to 1 in the 1930s, was reduced to less than 2 to 1, reflecting a return to the wage scales of 1928.[73]

Wage differentials both within the agricultural sector and between the agricultural and non-agricultural sectors were also sharply reduced. Up until the early 1950s there was a large gap between the incomes of agricultural and non-agricultural workers on the one hand, and between the incomes of the collective farmers and state-farm workers within the agricultural sector, on the other. But this gap was sharply reduced between 1955 and 1970. For instance, in 1950, the average annual income of collective farmers was less than 10 percent of that of agricultural workers on the state farms (42 rubles vs. 459 rubles); this gap was reduced to over 30 percent (221 rubles vs. 645 rubles) by 1960, 55 percent (483 rubles vs. 900 rubles) by 1965 and to 67 percent (1,027 rubles vs. 1,528 rubles) by 1975. By the same token, the average annual income of agricultural workers was increased from 11 percent of the income of non-agricultural workers (89 rubles vs. 830 rubles) in 1950 to 33 percent (330 rubles vs. 1,008 rubles) in 1960 and to 70 percent (1225 rubles vs. 1780 rubles) in 1975. In other words, between

[73] Sources: For 1928 and 1934 figures: A. Bergson, *op. cit.*, Appendix D, tables 9 and 10, pp. 227 and 223. For 1966 figures: P. J. D. Wiles and Stefan Arcowski, "Income Distribution Under Communism and Capitalism," Part 2, in *Soviet Studies*, Vol. 22, No. 4, April 1971, Table 28, p. 506. (Figures have been adjusted for the purpose of equalization of intervals.)

1955 and 1975, the average annual earnings of all agricultural workers in the Soviet Union were raised 3.6 times faster than the wages of all workers in the non-agricultural sectors.[74]

Such mechanical leveling of wages in such a short period of time (notwithstanding their phenomenal increase in absolute terms), which Stalin had declared "anti-Marxist and anti-Leninist" a few decades earlier, played the decisive role in reducing the rate of growth of production in the Soviet Union. More importantly, this was done at a time when, according to repeated assessments of the Party leadership, including the assessments of the June 1955 and July 1960 Plenums (both of which were held after the 21st Party Congress), the state had not been able to make much progress in introducing modern technology into the industries in order to increase labor productivity and capital efficiency. In fact, the initial growth of agricultural production during the years of 1954 to 1960 was not a result of increased productivity but mainly an outcome of Khrushchev's "Virgin Lands" project in which volunteers, mainly from the Communist Party's youth organization (Komsomol), fanned out into the countryside to cultivate 42 million hectares (nearly 104 million acres) of virgin and unused land. This initial growth, too, soon reached its limits, both due to the exhaustion of all uncultivated lands, which were cultivated within two or three years, and because of the adoption of certain incorrect agricultural policies by the Soviet leadership (such as growing corn for cattle feed). As a result, the average annual rate of growth of the Soviet Union's gross national product, which was about 15 percent during the decade of the 1940s, plummeted to 10 percent in the decade of the 1950s, and to 6.7 percent (less than half of the 1940s) between 1960 and 1972.[75]

Obviously, as it had also been emphasized by the 20th Congress of the CPSU, a drastic growth in the level of social

---

[74] Shroeder and Severin, *op. cit.*, p. 629.

[75] Gregory and Stuart, *op. cit.*, p. 378.

consumption as proposed by the economic plan, could only be achieved through a "continued growth of the heavy industry" as well as increased capital efficiency and labor productivity in both industry and agriculture which, in turn, depended heavily on the advancement of modern technology. The "rapid consumption growth" model, however, did the exact opposite. Rather than increasing the level of investments in heavy industry and focusing on technological modernization of the economy, it drastically increased the government's expenditures on consumption while at the same time reducing the relative share of capital investments in government expenditures. It sharply increased the working peoples' purchasing power without creating the material and technical capacity of the consumer goods industry. It mechanically levelled the wages throughout the economy and thus eliminated all the material incentives for increased production. And, finally, it created the ground for the growth of parasitic activities in society as well as corruption and bribery within the state bureaucracy. The combined effect of these misguided policies was the gradual emergence of a deep social and economic crisis in the Soviet Union.

What made this growing crisis inconspicuous back then was the apparent rise in the level of money wages and the relative increase in the degree of availability of consumer goods, mostly inspired by Western consumption patterns. The "rapid consumption growth" model gave rise to the illusion that, in just a few more years, the working people's standard of living and their level of consumption would catch up with the West, and would even surpass it. The hard reality, however, was that such a goal could be realized only in an advanced socialist society with a most technologically advanced productive infrastructure, and that Soviet society was still miles away from such a society. This subjective optimism was bound to be followed by mass disappointment.

2. The "Advanced Socialism" Model and the Grounds for Political Crisis

Undoubtedly in spite all these shortcomings, many of which were still due to the initial backwardness of Soviet society, the achievements of the "rapid consumption growth" model were impressive and resulted in a much higher growth rate compared to the capitalist economies. Modern technology, despite its lack of growth in the non-military industries, had big successes in the military sector. The Soviet Union demonstrated socialism's potential in science and technology when it launched its first satellite in October 1957. Socialist society had managed in a short period of time to raise the working peoples' standard of living in an unprecedented way, and to redress a major part of the shortcomings of the unbalanced industrial growth model.

But these advances, like in the previous models, had their own negative consequences, the elimination of which required a conscious and scientific approach on the part of the vanguard Party. Unfortunately, as the subsequent trends demonstrated, the Party not only failed to act effectively in undoing the newly emerged problems but by continuing to follow the economic guidelines of the "rapid consumption growth" model, it exacerbated the economic crisis. Moreover, the Party also took certain unrealistic political stands which helped to elevate the economic crisis to the political arena. These erroneous political decisions were founded not only on certain objective factors (which shall be discussed below) but primarily on a subjective exaggeration of the achievements of the socialist system.

The first signs of such subjectivist political approaches appeared in the Extraordinary 21st Congress of the Communist Party of the Soviet Union (January 27 to February 5, 1959). This Congress — dubbed as "a congress of builders of Communism"— while noting "with pride" that the Soviet Union "had blazed the trail to Socialism for mankind," concluded that "as a result of changes in all spheres of social life on the basis of victory of socialism," the Soviet Union "had entered a new period of its development, *the period of the full scale building of a Communist society." As* a result, "the principle of 'from each according to his ability, to each according to needs' would be gradually "applied at the higher stage of Communism."[76]

Based on its over-optimistic conclusions, not only did the Congress insist on the necessity of continuing the "rapid consumption growth" model, but it even expanded certain aspects of this model in many areas: The levelling of wages and the sharp wage increases across all sectors of the economy continued at an even faster pace, and the policy of directing state investments toward increased production of private consumption goods continued at an increasing rate. The inevitable result of such a policy was a persistent drop in the economic growth rate, especially in the industrial sector.

The declaration of the start of "the period of the full scale building of a Communist society" was more than anything else based on the comparison between socialism's growth rate and those of the capitalist societies at the time, as well as the immense credibility that such a growth had brought about for socialism and the Soviet Union worldwide. The roots of the emerging subjectivist approaches indeed lay in this superficial comparison. As a result, scientific assessment of the achievements and shortcomings of socialism within the context of its own predefined short-term and long-term objectives gave way to a competitive attitude based on comparing the achievements of socialism with those of the capitalist system which did not even pursue the same objectives as socialism. The outcome of such a comparison was obvious from the beginning: a sense of satisfaction, pride and exaggeration of the achievements of socialism on the one hand, while underestimating capitalism's economic potential and technological

---

[76] *History of the Communist party of the Soviet Union, op. cit.*, p. 719.

achievements, on the other.

The resolutions of the 22nd Congress of the Communist Party of the Soviet Union (October 1961) on the stage of development of socialist society in the Soviet Union were a true reflection of such subjectivist, optimistic tendencies within the Party's official outlook. The 22nd Congress, while putting a stamp of approval on the Party's actions since the 21st Congresses, and reiterating its belief in "the final and complete victory of socialism in the Soviet Union," declared that Soviet society had now entered the stage of advanced socialism and that it was embarking on the road "to building a communist society." Accordingly, the Congress approved the new (third) Party Program with the goal of "building a communist society" and "directed the Central Committee to mobilize the Party and the masses for carrying out the tasks of building communism and implementing the provisions of the seven-year plan as a major step for developing the material and technical foundation of communism."[77]

Obviously, adopting such a new and all-encompassing position about Soviet society entering the stage of building communism had certain economic, political, theoretical and even ideological consequences affecting all aspects of the Soviet society. As Marx had explained in his *Critique of the Gotha Programme,* the principles and requirements of building communism significantly differed from those of building socialism. Accordingly, priorities of economic planning; the structures and responsibilities of the Party and the state; the relationship between the Party and the class, and between the state and the people of the Soviet Union; and the role and function of the Soviet Union and the socialist bloc in the international arena of struggle against imperialism; all underwent major changes.

---

[77] *Ibid.,* p. 752.

Priorities of Economic Planning

Although, from an economic point of view, the "advanced socialist" model was based on the same principles as the "rapid consumption growth" model, declaring the start of the stage of "building communism" brought about serious changes in the priorities of economic planning, with lasting negative consequences. While in the previous model the issue of increased production (although with emphasis on consumption) was taken as the principal objective of economic planning, the new plan adopted by the 22nd Congress declared "improving the living standard of the people" as one of its principal objectives and outlined the mechanism for achieving this objective as follows:

> (a) raising individual payment according to the quantity and quality of work done, coupled with reduction of retail prices and abolition of taxes paid by the population; (b) increase of the public consumption fund intended for the satisfaction of the requirements of members of society irrespective of the quantity and quality of their labor, that is, free of charge....[78]

Adopting these mostly communistic mechanisms, at the time when the technical level of production and the level of labor productivity did not meet the material requirements of such a project, could only lead to economic problems. First, further increases in wages combined with reduced prices of goods, in a situation where the quantity and quality of consumer goods could not meet even the existing demand, would only result in further growth of the black market and expansion of the underground economy. Second, reducing the retail prices of commodities meant further increases in

---

[78] Programme of the Communist Party of the Soviet Union, adopted by the Twenty-Second Congress of the CPSU, October 31, 1961; reprinted in, Leonard Schapiro, ed., *The U.S.S.R. and the Future: An Analysis of the New Program of the CPSU*, Praeger, New York and London, 1963, Appendix A, p. 293.

state subsidies for consumer goods and hence an increase in state expenditures in the area of private consumption — a policy which clearly contradicted the stated goal of "increase in the public consumption fund." Third, the "abolition of taxes paid by the population," in addition to being another form of increase in people's disposable income that would further fuel the first problem, significantly reduced the government revenues. The state had always used taxes as a mechanism for directing private consumption patterns, and the elimination of taxes could only weaken the state's guiding role in this area. Finally, and perhaps most importantly, insisting on an "increase in the public consumption fund" for everyone "irrespective of the quantity and quality of their labor," in a situation where monetary wage differentials were being consciously reduced to a level even below that of the 1920's, would guarantee a universal material welfare without regard to the quantity of socially useful labor performed, thus further destroying material incentives for increased production.

This way, with the declaration of the start of "building communism," the whole mechanism of material incentives for work was transformed and weakened. The Communist method of reliance on subjective and moral motivations replaced the socialist mechanism of material incentives for work. This is clearly reflected in the program adopted by the 22nd Congress of the CPSU:

> In the struggle for the victory of communism, ideological work becomes an increasingly powerful factor. The higher the social consciousness of the members of society, the more fully and broadly their creative activities come into play in the building of the material and technical basis of communism, in the development of communist forms of labor and new relations between people....
>
> The Party considers that the paramount task in the present period is to educate all working people in the spirit of ideological integrity and devotion to communism, and cultivate in them a communist attitude to labor...; to

ensure the all-round, harmonious development of the individual; to create a truly rich spiritual culture....

The Party sees the development of a communist attitude to labor in all members of society as its chief educational task. Labor for the benefit of society is the sacred duty of all....

In the course of transition to communism, the moral principles of society become increasingly important; the sphere of action of the moral factor expands and the importance of the administrative control of human relations diminishes accordingly....

The Party holds that t*he moral code of the builder of communism* should comprise the following principles:

devotion to the communist cause, love of the socialist motherland and of the other socialist countries;

conscientious labor for the good of the society.... ;

concern on the part of everyone for the preservation and growth of public wealth;

a high sense of public duty; intolerance of actions harmful to the public interest;

collectivism and comradely mutual assistance: one for all and all for one;

humane relations and mutual respect between individuals... ;

honesty and truthfulness, moral purity, modesty, and unpretenciousness in social and private life; ...

an uncompromising attitude to injustice, parasitism, dishonesty, careerism and money grubbing;...[79]

Such elaborate inclusion, especially in the Party Program, of these moral principles — which have always been emphasized by Communists — not only reflected the growth of certain profiteering and careerist tendencies both within society and in the state organs as well as the need to confront them, but also manifested a shift in the Party's priorities away from the socialist principles of material incentives and

---

[79] *Ibid.*, pp. 303-304.

toward communist reliance on subjective and moral motivations. This shift, as the future trends would demonstrate, ironically led to a gradual growth of an attitude of indifference and laziness towards work, parasitism and, ultimately, a slowdown of economic growth. If one adds to these issues the technological shortcomings, the low quality of and lack of efficiency in production, the heavy expenditures on the cold war and the arms race imposed by imperialism, and the Soviet Union's tremendous international commitments to assist other socialist countries and national liberation movements, then one can better understand the crushing effects that such subjectivist policies bore on the socialist economy. The so-called "stagnation" crisis of the decade of the 70s, which is mostly associated with the Brezhnev period, was in fact a direct result of the 22nd Congress's subjectivist assessments of the stage of socialist development in the Soviet Union, and of the corresponding changes that were made in the priorities of the socialist system during that period.

The "State of the Entire People"

The declaration of the start of "building communism" in the Soviet Union brought about significant and serious changes in the political superstructure of society as well. This issue was especially decisive with regard to the character and the role of the state as well as its relationship to various social classes, and particularly to the working class.

The 22nd Congress [1961], on the basis of its new assessment of the stage of socialist development in the USSR, changed the character of the Soviet state from a "proletarian state" to a "state of entire people" and declared in its adopted program:

> [T]he dictatorship of the proletariat has fulfilled its historic mission and has ceased to be indispensable in the U.S.S.R. from the point of view of the tasks of internal development. The state, which arose as a state of the dicta-

torship of the proletariat, has, in the new, contemporary stage, become a state of the entire people, an organ expressing the interests and will of the people as a whole....[80]

This new approach to the character of the socialist state and the implicit annulment of the proletarian essence of the state was based on assumptions that did not correspond to the realities of society. Defining the state as the "organ expressing the interests and will of the people as a whole" could only be based on the premise that all objective differences among social classes in Soviet society had disappeared and that the Soviet people "as a whole" shared the same class interests. Such a premise, which denied the existence of classes and class struggle in a socialist society, was unjustified not only from the standpoint of the theory of socialism but also from an objective-historical point of view. From the theoretical point of view, Marx had clearly demonstrated that so long as all classes, including the proletariat itself, have not ceased to exist, the socialist state would have a class character and that the working-class must have hegemony over the state power. There can be no doubt that the CPSU leadership was fully aware of this fact, especially since in the same program it was emphasized that "the working class is the foremost and best organized force of Soviet society," and that "it plays also a leading role in the period of the full-scale construction of communism."[81]

On the other hand, the historical differences among various social classes, which had manifested themselves in many ways throughout the history of socialism, had not dissipated. The Congress still correctly insisted on the need for unity among workers, peasants and intellectuals as an important factor in the process of building socialism and considered this unity as the key to socialism's success. Obviously, were

---

[80] *Ibid.*, p. 297.

[81] *Ibid.*

these classes sharing the same interests, establishing unity among them would not have been considered as one of the main arenas of struggle for the Party.

In light of these facts, it would be wrong to assume that declaring the establishment of the "state of the entire people" independent of the interests of any particular class — a concept that was in clear violation of the theoretical principles of socialism as well as the existing class realities — was merely a result of subjective idealism on the part of the CPSU leadership. On the contrary, the actual root of this incorrect assessment must be found in the growth and gradual strengthening of bureaucratic and technocratic layers, which had taken charge of the state especially during the period of "rapid industrialization" when the administrative control of the economy had become a historical necessity for the Soviet state.

In fact, the idea of a class-independent state, especially the idea of the relative autonomy of the socialist state from the working class, was put forth by people like Malenkov during the first few years following Stalin's death (1954-56) and even led to confrontations and purges within the Party. Khrushchev's steps to limit the power of the state bureaucracy and the "technocratic counterrevolution" during those years succeeded to slow this trend to a certain degree. But the growing state bureaucracy, which, after the 20th Congress, had acquired material and economic incentives in addition to its hunger for power, increasingly questioned the Party's supervision of the state. Unfortunately, the lack of a deep-rooted and structural approach to this problem by the 20th Congress, which limited its discussions to a criticism of "Stalin's personality cult," perpetuated this trend and further weakened the Party *vis-a-vis* the growing state bureaucracy. Certain incorrect economic policies, which during the era of "rapid industrialization" had increasingly led to unproductive economic activities, bringing illegal incomes and privileges to the upper levels of the state bureaucracy, had also played a major role in the strengthening of these layers within the state.

If these analyses are correct, then the decisions of the 22nd Congress of the CPSU must be viewed as a clear sign of the domination of the state bureaucracy's outlook over socialism's political structures, and a major historical turning point in the course of socialist development in the Soviet Union. For the first time in the history of socialism, politics had come to rule over the theory and ideology of the proletariat, placing both at its own service. This signified the reversal of the relationship between the Party and the state and the actual dominance of the latter over the former. It tremendously weakened the proletarian leadership in socialist society and paved the way for an undisputed domination of the state bureaucracy's interests and outlook over all aspects of socialist society.

The consequences of the change in the character of the socialist state were important and decisive. By obscuring class distinctions, the "state of the entire people" lost its immunity against non-proletarian worldviews and gravitated more and more towards bureaucratization. The interests of the working class and of other toiling classes were increasingly overshadowed by those of the state bureaucracy. Socialist democracy gave way to a formal and bureaucratic democracy. Bureaucratic corruption and abuse of power and office for economic and political gains became widespread. In the absence of material class incentives, creativity and diligence at work gave way to laziness and complacency. This phenomenon increasingly caused the Party and state's economic plans to be delayed, projects to remain unfinished, or in some cases (such as the plan for the development of modern technology and its wide application in industry) to come to a complete halt.

All of this was happening at the time when the imperialist states, especially the United States, were using all their financial might and advanced technological capabilities to intensify their cold-war, anti-communist propaganda against the Soviet Union, bombarding the working people of the USSR with their ideological broadcasts through radio, television and other means of mass communication. The combined effect of these internal and external factors was the increasing alienation of the working people of the Soviet Union from the Party and state, and the preparation of the grounds for the emergence of a political crisis in the socialist society.

The "Party of the Entire People"

Such dominance of bureaucratic interests and outlook over socialism's political structures not only changed the relationship between the Party and the state but also weakened the proletarian essence and composition of the vanguard Party through the infiltration of these interests and outlooks into the Party itself. The CPSU Programme and Bylaws approved by the 22nd Congress in 1961 declared:

> As a result of the victory of socialism in the U.S.S.R. and the consolidation of the unity of Soviet society, the Communist Party of the working class has become the vanguard of the Soviet people, a Party of the entire people....[82]

The Congress, through changing the Party's by-laws, defined the "main criterion for membership in the Party" as "active participation in building communism."[83] In doing so, the Congress not only undermined the Party's working-class character but removed all class criteria for membership in the Party as well.

This was in clear violation of the Leninist ideological and organizational principles of a working class Party of a new type, with serious consequences that eventually disarmed the Party and forced it into submission before the growing weight

---

[82] *Ibid.*, p. 310.

[83] *Ibid.*

128

of the bureaucratic and technocratic layers. Although the 23rd Congress of the CPSU (held March 29 to April 8, 1966) adopted measures to correct "the subjectivist errors in the methods of leadership in changing without reason the methods of work in the Party, the economy and the councils,"[84] and changed the Party by-laws to make membership criteria more stringent, these measures did not go as far as reversing the new characterization of the Party as the "Party of the entire People"— a characterization which continued until the political crisis of the mid-1980s. Indeed, the Seventh (Special) Session of the Supreme Soviet of the USSR ratified the concept of the "State of the Entire People," adding it to the country's new constitution in October 1977.

In this manner, the transformation of the political Party of the working class into a "Party of the entire people" and the opening of its doors to whoever was "actively participating in building communism" — i.e., all those employed in society regardless of their class base and class position — opened the gates wide for the entry of careerist state bureaucrats into the Party. In fact, the rapid rise in the Party membership between the 20th Congress (1956) and the 22nd Congress (1961) and thereafter, was more a sign of the deluge of the state bureaucrats into the Party than a manifestation of an increased working class participation in Party life. While between the 17th and the 19th Congresses (1934-1952), i.e., in a span of 18 years, membership in the Party had increased by only 4 million (from 1.9 million in 1934 to 6 million in 1952), the membership increased to 6.8 million by 1956 (20th Congress), 11.7 million by 1966 (23rd Congress), 13.8 million by 1971 (24th Congress), 15.7 million by 1976 (25th Congress)[85] and more than 19 million by 1986 (27th Congress). In other words, more than 13 million had joined

---

[84] *History of the Communist Party of the Soviet Union*, Farsi ed., Tudeh Party of Iran Publications, 1979, p. 796.

[85] *Ibid.*, pages 542, 687, 719, 793, 852, and 917.

the Party between the 20th and the 27th Congresses — 4 million during the 1959-1966 period alone!

Given the Party's membership criteria during those years, it is clear that this rapid growth in numbers was not in the direction of strengthening the Party's working class base. Rather, it was a clear manifestation of the growth of the bureaucratic and technocratic layers within the Party ranks. While by the end of 1970, workers made up 57 percent of the country's total population, their share in the total Party membership was only 40 percent. By the same token, the peasants, who constituted 20 percent of the total population, made up only 13 percent of the Party membership.[86] On the other hand, by the same year, intellectuals and bureaucrats constituted less than 20 percent of the country's total population while they made up nearly half the Party's membership. Still, their share in the Party's leadership positions was much higher than their share in its total membership. According to the CPSU's own report, by the beginning of 1971, nearly all of the Party's CC secretaries at the level of the republics, as well as secretaries of the Party's provincial, regional, municipal and district committees were graduates of institutions of higher education, and more than half of them were engineers, economic and technical experts and agricultural engineers.[87] One can assume that many of these people were joining the Party not out of ideological convictions — which were being eroded over time throughout the society anyhow — but in search of special economic privileges and political leadership positions that Party membership brought for them.

The blurring of the structural distinctions between the Party and the state was the main cause of the growing influence of bureaucratic outlook and careerism within the Party. Many of the top Party leaders and cadres had government positions

---

[86] *Ibid.*, p. 823.

[87] Ibid., p. 827

and, in addition to their political responsibilities, were also in charge of managing the country's economy. This phenomenon, which had originated during the Stalin era with the implementation of the "rapid industrialization" model, expanded during the Khrushchev era as well, despite the latter's declared campaign against the state bureaucracy.

The confluence of the Party and the state structures not only created lucrative material incentives for joining the Party but also increasingly tied the Party's interests with those of the state bureaucracy in maintaining the status quo. Political and economic pragmatism gradually replaced creativity, innovativeness and farsightedness. The Communists' historical mission of constant "abolishing of the present state of things" was being increasingly contradicted by the bureaucratic incentive to "keep the existing personal privileges." This phenomenon was perhaps more prevalent among the Party intellectuals who, instead of continually analyzing the situation and showing the ways out of the problems, increasingly placed their theoretical capabilities at the service of praising the status quo and justifying the policies and actions of the state bureaucracy.

Thus, while the Party was correctly emphasizing the need to intensify ideological training of its members and working people in the society, the trends within the Party itself were moving in the opposite direction, further weakening its proletarian character. Working class ideology was gradually transformed into a hollow outer shell, inside which the growing parasitic and opportunist bureaucratic layers were eating away the Party's vitality and strength. The vanguard Party was increasingly distanced from its historical responsibilities and from the class it represented. And socialist society, despite all its immense and historic achievements, was being dragged into a general political and economic crisis.

3. Socialism, Imperialism and World Revolution

The 22nd Congress's optimistic analysis of the stage of socialist development in the Soviet Union was accompanied by the declaration that the socialist system had overtaken the capitalist system. Based on this view, the Congress declared in its platform that "the third stage of crisis for capitalism has started," and that this crisis is going to destroy capitalism completely:

> Imperialism has entered the period of decline and collapse. An inexonerable process of decay has seized capitalism from top to bottom.... Imperialism has for ever lost its power over the bulk of mankind....
>
> ... *the world imperialist system is rent by deep-rooted and acute contradictions.* The antagonism of labor and capital, the contradictions between the people and the monopolies, growing militarism, the break-up of the colonial system, the contradictions between the imperialist countries, conflicts and contradictions between the young national states and those of the old colonial powers, and — most important of all — the rapid growth of world socialism, are sapping and destroying imperialism, leading to its weakening and collapse.[88]

And from this analysis, it concluded that:

> As a result of the devoted labor of the Soviet people, and the theoretical and practical activities of the Communist Party of the Soviet Union ... *the highroad to socialism has been paved.* Many peoples are already marching along it, and it will be taken sooner or later by all peoples.[89]

One year earlier, in November 1960, similar views were

---

[88] Programme of the Communist Party of the Soviet Union, *op. cit.*, pp. 268, 271.

[89] *Ibid.*, p. 265.

expressed by the "Consultative Meeting of the World Communist and Workers Parties" in Moscow with the participation of 81 parties. The declaration issued from this meeting stated that "our period ... is a period of the downfall of imperialism ... period of continual transition of the masses to the road of socialism and of global victory for socialism and communism." While emphasizing "the increasing shift in the balance of forces in favor of socialism," the declaration noted that "in the current period ... the world socialist system and the forces who struggle against imperialism and for the socialist transformation of society determine the main character and direction of the historical development of the human society."[90] The Consultative Meeting of the Communist Parties went so far in its overly optimistic view as to declare that "the colonial system of imperialism has completely disintegrated under the blows of the national liberation movements."[91] The same optimistic view was expressed by the 22nd Congress of the CPSU when it stressed that "imperialism had been weakened and the balance of forces had tilted in favor of socialism."[92]

There is no doubt that socialism's tremendous domestic and international achievements were the objective ground for such optimism. Popular revolution under the leadership of Communists had succeeded in China. The socialist countries of eastern Europe, with the help of the Soviet Union, were taking rapid steps in the direction of strengthening their economic-industrial infrastructure and building socialism. And the national liberation movements, inspired by and relying on the achievements of socialism, were growing in strength throughout the world, attaining new victories each passing day. All these developments supported such an

---

[90] *Ibid.*, pp. 747-748.

[91] *Ibid.* p. 749.

[92] Programme of the Communist Party of the Soviet Union, *op. cit.*, p. 266.

optimistic view of the future.

But the optimism about the "smoothness" of the "highroad to socialism" and the "continual march of the masses to the road of socialism" and the immanent "global victory of socialism and communism" was based on two important assumptions: first, the inability of the capitalist system to delay the fatal impact of its "general crisis;" and second, the continued rapid development of the socialist societies in the sphere of economic production, and especially in the area of technical and technological modernization. Experience, however, showed that both assumptions, which were not totally unrelated, were based on an inaccurate assessment of reality.

Marxist analysis of the capitalist system has produced an accurate account of the nature of the growing "general crisis" of capitalism. However, this characteristic feature of capitalism, the inevitability of which has been proved, had lulled many Marxist-Leninists into believing that this crisis would in and of itself lead to capitalism's "disintegration" without any conscious, planned and coordinated effort by the working class and its allies worldwide. They mistakenly equated the inevitability of the capitalist "crisis" with the certainty of its "disintegration" and collapse, and thus ignored the possibility that capitalism, in spite of its general crisis, could continue its existence by relying on its sheer economic power and its modern production technology. Reality also showed that capitalism, despite its growing general crisis, was able to regenerate itself and, at least at this juncture, escape the abyss of annihilation by intensifying its exploitation of workers and spreading poverty and deprivation for billions of people in all corners of the world.

The tendency towards presuming that capitalism's downfall is inevitable and that its collapse is just a matter of time led to an underestimation of capitalism's ability to survive in the face of growing socialism. The analysts in the socialist world underestimated the impact of capitalism's technological revolution during the decades of the 1970s and the 1980s as well as the structural changes that were carried out during the 1970s to reduce the effects of capitalism's general crisis and to prevent its demise.

This underestimation was a result not only of the incorrect assumptions about the inevitability of capitalism's collapse but also of the unrealistic assessment about the shift in the world balance of forces in favor of socialism. While capitalism was exporting its crisis into the socialist societies through the intensification of the arms race and imposition of heavy military expenditures on socialism — expenditures which hindered socialism's balanced growth by forcing its limited financial and technical resources into the area of military production — the Party leadership still insisted on its optimistic assessment at the end of the 1960s that imperialism "has not been able to delay the economic development of the socialist countries."[93] This claim was being made at the time when, according to the Soviet comrades' own admission, "between 1965-1970, the United States had spent close to $400 billion for military purposes" and "NATO's military budget in 1970 exceeded $100 billion."[94] The fact that the Soviet Union's total gross national product in 1971 was less than $549 billion indicates the unrealistic nature and overly optimistic extent of the claim about the shift in the world balance of forces in favor of socialism.

It was based on these overly optimistic assessments of socialism's economic power and the total disregard for capitalism's immense economic and technological capability that, during the 1960s, 1970s and the early 1980s, the Soviet Union was dragged into an expensive and destructive arms race on the one hand, and huge international economic and military commitments that were far beyond its realistic ability, on the other. Although a large part of these military expendi-

---

[93] *History of the Communist Party of the Soviet Union*, Farsi ed., Tudeh Party of Iran Publications, 1979, p. 849.

[94] *Ibid.*, p. 847.

tures and economic assistance to other socialist countries and the liberation movements were necessary, a more realistic approach to the abilities of the socialist system could have reduced the burden and thus limited the pressure on socialism and the working people of the socialist countries.

The fact was that by the late 1960s and the early 1970s, the Soviet Union had managed to reach a relative military parity with the West, albeit by having incurred heavy expenditures. This parity had brought the necessary guarantees for the "survival of socialism" against the danger of imperialist aggression. The Communist Party's assessments also confirmed this view:

> But the historical events of the 1960s had shown that imperialism was incapable of changing the world situation in its own favor and reversing the course of its progress....
>
> Capitalism's ability to use its military power for aggressive purposes had been limited to a great degree. The time had passed when the United States could, by having stationed bomber planes equipped with nuclear weapons in military bases of countries around the Soviet Union and other socialist countries, threaten these countries and be immune to retaliation. In the 1960s, the Soviet Union had enough nuclear weapons and inter-continental ballistic missiles to inflict reciprocal blows on any aggressor in any part of the world.[95]

Based on this evaluation, it would be expected that the Soviet Union would reduce its military expenditures and redirect its internal resources towards expanding the non-military and technologically advanced industries. However, this did not happen, and despite all the persistent and admirable efforts of the Soviet Union and the other socialist countries in trying to end the arms race, the military expenditures kept rising in competition with imperialism. By 1977, the Soviet state was spending more than $52 billion annually on

---

[95] *Ibid.*, p. 849.

military expenditures.[96] Although the absolute amounts of these expenditures were still far less than those of the United States ($100.9 billion)[97] and therefore of all the imperialist countries combined, the smaller size of the Soviet economy in comparison to that of the imperialist countries and especially of the United States (in 1971, the Soviet Union's gross national product was less than 55 percent of that of the United States — $548.6 billion vs. $1000.4 billion),[98] made the share of these expenditures in the Soviet economy extremely high, putting a much heavier burden on the socialist system. By imposing such an expensive arms race on the socialist countries while gaining huge profits from it, imperialism was in fact exploiting the working people of the socialist countries from outside their borders. And this was not a burden that the socialist system, the balanced and persistent growth of which significantly depended on peace, could carry on its shoulders for a long period of time.

On the other hand, unlike the imperialist states, the socialist system could not base its foreign trade on the exploitation of other nations. The Soviet Union's trade relations with the "Third World" countries and the national liberation movements were based on assisting their economic development and providing them with military and economic aid. Naturally, these commitments put a heavy economic burden on socialism. In the 1970s and thereafter, nearly 10 percent of the Soviet government's annual budget was allocated to international assistance for the other socialist countries and the national liberation movements around the world. As Robert McNamara, US Secretary of Defense in the Kennedy Administration, commented:

---

[96] Stockholm International Peace Research Institute (SIPRI), *World Armament and Disarmament: SIPRI Yearbook,* 1977; Quoted in M. Myerson and M. Solomon, *Stopping World War III,* US Peace Council, New York, 1981, p. 72.

[97] *Ibid.*

[98] Gregory and Stuart, *op. cit.*, Table 1, p. 3.

The United States sells many of its expensive weapons to its wealthy friends in, for instance, the Middle East. The Soviet Union is forced to sell its weapons cheaply to its "fighting" friends. Accordingly, the United States' friends will be an additional source of income while the Soviets' friends are a heavy burden for them.[99]

The correctness and necessity of such assistance could not, and cannot, be doubted by anyone. However, their continuation and expansion necessitated further strengthening of the Soviet economy, especially its industrial output, through directing some of the investments away from the military sector and towards the industrial and the technological sectors. The arms race imposed by imperialism, however, prevented this. In fact, imperialism's military strategy against the Soviet Union was devised exactly with these constraints of the Soviet Union's socialist economy in mind. Again, Robert McNamara described the American strategy for the arms race as follows:

> The Soviet Union came out of the Second World War with a brilliant military victory. With heavy casualty and high economic expenditure ..., this country had three priorities for its plan after the war: 1. Renewing the country's infrastructure completely so the Soviet people could reach the promise of communism; 2. Rebuilding and renewing the country's defenses in face of the stalking capitalist world; 3. Gaining new friends in the world, especially in Eastern Europe and the Third World....
>
> If the United States succeeds in engaging the Soviet Union in an arms race, then all these plans would go out the window.... Our goal was very simple: the second priority would, if possible, replace the first priority. In other words, first increasing the military expenditures and last, improving the people's standard of living... and of course this would affect the third priority as well.
>
> What is the meaning of this? It means that if the Soviet

---

[99] Mohammad Hassanin Heikal, *Revisiting History,* tr. by Hassan Faramarzi, Hafteh Publications, Tehran, 1990, p. 21.

Union is dragged into an arms race and a massive portion of its budget, 40 percent if possible, is allocated to this purpose, then a lesser amount would be left for improving the people's lives, and therefore, the dream of communism, which so many people are awaiting around the world, would be postponed and the friends of the Soviet Union and the supporters of the idea of communism would have to wait a long time.... On the basis of this calculation, the arms race may even threaten Soviet ideology in Moscow itself.[100]

It is obvious that the only way to frustrate this anti-human and anti-communist strategy of imperialism was for the Soviet Union to reduce its military expenditures once military parity had been achieved in the late 1960s. At the same time, it is clear that no degree of optimism could have prevented the Soviet leadership from seeing the true nature and objective of the arms race and its destructive consequences for socialism, the effects of which had already surfaced in the economy.

The main cause of the increase in the Soviet Union's military expenditures after the decade of the 1960s must be sought not simply in the Party leadership's optimistic attitudes but in the interests of the growing layers of state bureaucracy. From the state bureaucracy's point of view, the arms race was more of a rivalry between the governments of the Soviet Union and the West, particularly the United States, than an historical struggle for survival between the socialist and capitalist systems. This bureaucratic layer placed its own interests ahead of the long-term interests of the Party and socialism, and acted accordingly. Indeed, the continuation of the arms race and the increasing allocation of funds to the military sector would only strengthen the state apparatus as a base of power for these bureaucratic layers. It would also strengthen them economically and politically. That is why this growing layer not only had no incentive for reducing socialism's mil-

---

[100] *Ibid.*, pp. 210-211.

itary expenditure but actually considered such a policy contrary to its own objective interests. It was thus that imperialism succeeded in imposing on socialism its military and arms race strategy to the point of "threatening Soviet ideology even in Moscow," and hence postponing the world revolution for a significant period of time.

4. Proletarian Internationalism and the Relationship Among the Parties

The continual and unchecked growth of the bureaucratic layers within the socialist state, the increasing confluence of the Party and the state structures, and the eventual reversal of the relationship between of the Party and the state, the natural outcome of which was the gradual replacement of theoretical creativity and ideological farsightedness by political pragmatism, left lasting marks on the international relations between the Communist Party of Soviet Union and the other Communist parties as well. Due to the special stature of the state and the Communist Party of the Soviet Union, this issue took on an even larger scale, affecting the relationship among all the Communist and Workers' parties around the world.

The most important aspect of this situation was its effect on the concept of "proletarian internationalism." The dominance of the state bureaucracy's outlook over socialism's political structures transformed the concept of "proletarian internationalism" from a fraternal relationship of international solidarity among the Communist and Workers' Parties to a relationship of solidarity with the socialist states. This had serious negative consequences for the world Communist and working-class movement in several important respects:

First, the relationship among the Communist and Workers parties around the world was overshadowed by the relationship between states. This issue clearly manifested itself particularly in the emerging differences between the Soviet Union and China. Although, at first, differences arose between the two parties, one cannot doubt that the actual reason for the conflict was the policy differences between the two states, especially in relation to their respective approach to imperialist countries. The emergence of a phenomenon known as "Maoism," which characterized the Soviet Union as a "social imperialist state" and the "peoples' main enemy" without any scientific or historical justification, and the rift it created within the world Communist movement, cannot simply be attributed to the differences between two fraternal Communist parties. The CPSU was carrying on the struggle for socialism in the most difficult conditions under the siege of imperialism, and no political difference should have been accorded higher priority than the urgent need for maintaining unity within the world Communist movement.

The spillover of these differences to many of the Communist and Workers' parties, which led to repeated splits within these parties and the emergence of new dividing lines within the communist movement was a clear indication of the fact that the criterion of "international solidarity with the socialist states" had replaced the principle of "international solidarity among the Communist parties." Not only did this seriously damage the capability of the Communist and Workers' parties in their common struggle against capitalism and imperialism, but also diverted a considerable portion of the two country's financial, military and propaganda capabilities and resources away from their common struggle against imperialism and toward struggle against each other. Undoubtedly, imperialism was the biggest winner in this process. The imperialist states took utmost advantage of the differences between China and the Soviet Union and the ensuing splits within the world Communist movement to further weaken socialism in all countries.

The fading of the lines of demarcation between the Party

141

and the state structures in the socialist countries also provided imperialism with new opportunities for anti-communist propaganda. The imperialist media and its propaganda machine presented the international solidarity among the Communist and Workers' parties as a sign of their "dependence" on the socialist states, especially on the Soviet state, and labelled these parties as the "fifth columns" and "spies" for the socialist governments. The confluence of the Party and the state structures in the socialist countries made it even more difficult for the Communist and Workers' parties to fight off these unfounded allegations. This issue also prevented the working people of the capitalist countries, who were and still are under the heavy influence of the ruling bourgeoisie's nationalist ideology and propaganda, from joining the Communist and Workers' parties in their own countries. This trend, in the long term, weakened the mass base of the labor and communist movements in capitalist countries.

Secondly, as the Communist task of constant "abolishing of the present state of things," the theoretical critique of the existing shortcomings gave way to a bureaucratic praise and justification of the status quo, and the assessments of the world Communist and Workers' parties of the weaknesses of "real existing socialism" became ever less critical. The general policy of not weakening the socialist states in the face of imperialist propaganda took center stage in the activities of the world Communist and Workers' movement. Thus, the theoretical and ideological task of upholding the scientific principles of socialism and communism against all deviations and distortions gradually lost its significance before the more urgent political responsibility of defending "real existing socialism" *vis-a-vis* capitalism and imperialism. In many instances, calculated silence in the face of socialist societies' shortcomings not only became the dominant policy for many Communist and Workers' parties but adherence to this policy became a gauge for measuring a party's commitment to the cause of the working class and Communism.

142

Criticizing the weaknesses of "real existing socialism" was increasingly viewed as opposition to "socialism," and the dogmatic attitude of "whoever is not with us is against us" became the dominant attitude in some parties. This undoubtedly kept many sincere people, who were committed to the ideals of Communism but could not accept the shortcomings of the existing socialist systems, away from the Communist parties, thus further contributing to the fragmentation of the Communist movement.

However, the two political and theoretical responsibilities of communists were not antithetical but essentially complementary. Just as a theoretical critique of the weaknesses of "real existing socialism" could not and should not have prevented the Communists from providing a firm and unconditional support for these societies in the face of military aggression and propaganda campaigns of the imperialist countries, similarly, the defense of the socialist societies could not and should not have negated the Communists' responsibility for a theoretical critique of these systems. Confusing these two equally important tasks and placing the political responsibilities above the theoretical and ideological ones was the main source of the growth of political pragmatism within the Communist and Workers' movement. It prevented the Communists from a timely diagnosis of the weaknesses of "existing socialism" and taking steps to correct them. Lack of a theoretical and ideological approach to the weaknesses of the existing socialist systems further paved the way for an unchecked growth of bureaucratic layers within the structures of the socialist states and the ruling parties.

Thus, the subjective errors of the vanguard Party in the course of three decades contributed to the weakening and increased vulnerability of the world Communist and working-class movement in the face of imperialism's economic, military and propaganda onslaught, and created favorable grounds for the emergence of a serious crisis in the socialist countries.

143

However, as Lenin had correctly emphasized, the mere existence of objective conditions could not in and of itself lead to a political crisis and hence to the collapse of the socialist system. Such a development would require the presence of certain subjective factors, including an organized and conscious mobilization against socialism by those who benefited from its dismantling.

One such factor, imperialism, had for seven decades used all the means at its disposal to disrupt and, if possible, topple the socialist system, constantly acting as the main source of its emerging crisis. But imperialism could not achieve its ultimate goal because it lacked an internal support base within the socialist system itself. In all previous decades, especially after the victory of the October Revolution and during World War II, when the conditions were far more severe and socialism was much weaker than in the 1980s, the socialist state had heroically defended itself and had overcome all its internal and external enemies. Despite all external pressures and internal shortcomings, the socialist system had also managed to overcome periodic crises caused by its growth and development through making the necessary changes to its social structure and adopting socioeconomic models that corresponded to its objective conditions.

Despite all its shortcomings, socialism had amassed enough impressive and unprecedented historical achievements to carry it through the latest crisis as well, and to guarantee its continued march towards a Communist society. Socialism had not only achieved its military security *vis-a-vis* imperialism but had also succeeded in forcing the latter to sign several nuclear test ban treaties and reduce its nuclear weapons stockpile. Socialism had developed its economic and industrial infrastructure, raised its share in the world's total industrial output to more than one third, and surpassed capitalism in many areas of industry, science and technology. Socialism had impressively improved the standard of living of the working people; had guaranteed free education and health for all; had eradicated illiteracy and unemployment; and had developed a highly educated and skilled working class. Socialism had taken the masses to a very high level of education and culture, and had given to twentieth century humanity some of its most prominent writers, poets and artists. Socialism had established peaceful coexistence among different nationalities living within its borders. On a global scale, socialism had played a decisive role in the downfall of the old colonial system; in the liberation of the oppressed peoples of Asia, Africa and Latin America; and in the struggles of many nations for political independence and socioeconomic development. And finally, despite all imperialist subversions, military aggression and economic and technological blockades, socialism had enjoyed a long-term economic growth rate much higher than those of the most advanced capitalist countries.

Socialism's crisis was a crisis of growth, not of failure. At every stage of its development, socialism had to adjust its social and economic relations of production to the new level of development of its productive forces in order to guarantee its continued growth. What transformed this natural crisis of growth into an objective ground for a socio-political crisis were the subjective errors of the CPSU and the lack of timely actions to readjust the relations of production to socialism's newly developed productive forces.

Still, none of these errors were enough to topple the socialist order. Sufficient resources were still available to correct the mistakes, and socialism could still rely on its achievements to eliminate the grounds of the crisis. What prevented this and pushed the turn of events towards the dismantling of the socialist system was the emergence, growth and ultimate betrayal of socialism by a certain social layer which, to advance its own narrow interests, both in the Party and in the state, actually became the internal base for imperialism's plots against socialism, thus providing the former with the necessary political tools to destroy socialism from within.

145

Part Four:

From Renewal to Dismantling of Socialism

1. The Initial Phase of Transformations

The grounds for the crisis, which had been long in the making, and which were well in evidence by the 1970s, finally impelled the Soviet leadership in the 1980s to confront the problems and seek out actual solutions. The genesis of this approach was the election of Yuri Andropov to the post of the Party's General Secretary, which took place at the Central Committee's November 12th, 1982 Plenum after the passing of Leonid Brezhnev. Ten days later, Andropov declared at the November 22nd Plenum of the Central Committee that: "by a number of key indicators the targets of the first two years of the [11th] five year period were not fulfilled," and that the "chief indicator of the economy's efficiency — labor productivity — is growing at a rate which is unsatisfactory for us." He went on to say that: "There are still many economic managers who, while readily quoting Leonid Brezhnev's famous words that the economy should be economical, are doing little in practice to achieve this." On the basis of these observations, he called for a major overhaul of the country's economic organization. Some of the highlights of his proposals were as follows:

• It is necessary to create the economic and organizational conditions to encourage quality workmanship, productivity, initiative and enterprise. Conversely, shoddy work, inactivity and irresponsibility should have an immediate and unavoidable effect on a worker's remuneration, official status and moral prestige....

• It is necessary to raise responsibility for observing the interests of the whole state and the whole people, and resolutely to root out departmentalism and parochialism. Every breach of party, state and labor discipline should be combatted more resolutely....

• We have large reserves in the national economy.... These reserves are to be found in the speeding up of scientific and technological progress and in the large-scale and speedy introduction of scientific and technological achievements and advanced experience in production. This question is not new, of course.... Nevertheless, progress is slow....

• The joining of science and production should be promoted by planning methods and by the system of material incentives....

• The task is not only to increase the production of consumer goods but also to improve their quality considerably. This applies not only to light and local industries but also to the enterprises in the heavy and defense industries....

• We have quite a few examples of creative work and of a truly thrifty attitude to the people's property, but unfortunately this experience is not properly disseminated.... This means that something else is lacking, namely, initiative and resolute struggle against mismanagement and wastefulness....

• One of the central tasks in the national economy is to introduce order in capital construction.... A steady rise of the economy and improvement of the people's welfare are both our duty to the Soviet people and our internationalist duty. In posing the question in this way the party is guided by Lenin's far-sighted statement that we exercise our main influence on the world revolutionary process through our economic policy.

• We think that the difficulties and tension characteristic

of the present international situation can and must be overcome. Humankind cannot keep on putting up with the arms race and with wars if it does not want to jeopardize its future. The CPSU does not want the dispute of ideas to grow into a confrontation between states and peoples; it does not want arms and the readiness to use them to become a gauge of the potentials of the social systems... military rivalry is not our choice; socialism's ideal is a world without arms.

• I would like to stress that these questions are of primary importance and vital to the country. If we resolve them successfully, the economy will continue to grow and the people's living standards will be further improved....

• Of course, this task can only be accomplished with the participation of every worker and everyone working at our enterprises and collective and state farms. We should strive to ensure that they see this task as their own cause....[101]

Andropov correctly identified the root cause of social problems that were gripping and weakening the socialist system as the problem of income "levelling" that had eroded material incentives for work. He warned that the levelling of wages had given rise to the growth of "parasitic phenomena" on the "humane body of socialism."

Later, in March 1983, in a famous speech made on the 100th anniversary of the death of Karl Marx,[102] referring to Marx's theory of distribution in the initial phases of communism, he insisted that: "It is work and work alone, its actual results and not somebody's subjective desire or goodwill which should determine the level of material well-being of every citizen." He stressed that any attempt "to lunge ahead — to communist forms of distribution — without accurately assessing the labor contribution made by each person" is bound to create "unearned incomes, so-called rolling stones,

---

[101] *Information Bulletin*, Documents of the Communist and Workers' Parties, Peace and Socialism Publishers, Prague, January 1983, pp. 7-10.

[102] *Information Bulletin*, May 1983, pp. 3-11.

shirkers, slackers, and bad workers who really sponge on society and live off the mass of conscientious workers."[103] In his speech, Andropov declared "any violation of the objective economic requirement for a more rapid growth in labor productivity than in consumption" as being "inadmissible." In his words, "a wage increase which is not very closely related to this decisive factor eventually has a negative effect on the entire economic life. Specifically, it stimulates demands which cannot be fully satisfied at the given level of production and hampers steps to eliminate shortages with all their ugly consequences, justly resented by the working people."[104] Moreover, while blaming the low level of labor productivity on the lack of application of modern technology to the production process, he insisted that "it is impermissible from an economic point of view to maintain the considerable share of manual, non-mechanized labor, which stands at 40 percent in industry alone."[105] On this basis, he warned "against possible exaggerations of the extent to which [the Soviet Union] has neared the highest phase of communism." He stressed that "we must have a sober idea of where we are. To run ahead means to put forward unfeasible tasks; to be content with what has been achieved means to fail to use everything at our disposal. What is now required is to see our society in real dynamics, with all its potentialities and needs."[106]

Andropov pointed to some important political and ideological issues that had been ignored for a long time. While endorsing the concept of the "state of all people," he pointed out that the establishment of socialism is "inconceivable without ... the dictatorship of proletariat." Referring to Marx's teaching, he stressed that "it is this dictatorship which opens the road of political development ultimately leading to com

---

[103] *Ibid*, p. 6.

[104] *Ibid.*

[105] *Ibid*, p. 7.

[106] *Ibid.*

munist self-government."[107] He openly declared that "Soviet democracy has been having ... and is still going to have difficulties of growth" as a result of numerous factors including "the 'psychological war' unleashed by imperialism," and insisted that its improvement "requires the elimination of bureaucratic overorganization and formalism" and "everything which dampens and undermines the initiative of the masses, shackles creative thinking and the living cause of the working people."[108] He emphasized that "the proven organizational principle of the entire life of socialist society is democratic centralism, which makes it possible to combine successfully the advantages of a single system of scientific guidance, planning and management.... But unfortunately there are still people who try to oppose their selfish interests to society, to its other members. In this light it is becoming clear that it is necessary to work to educate, sometimes re-educate, some persons, and to combat the encroachments on socialist law and order and norms of collectivist life. And this is not 'flouting of human rights' ... but real humanism and democracy, which mean administration by will of the majority and in the interests of all the working people."[109]

Andropov characterized the idea that socialism "gets rid of every single contradiction and difference" as "simplistic and politically naive" and conceded that Soviet society has "both contradictions and difficulties." In his view, the fact that antagonistic contradictions do not exist in socialism should not lead to the conclusion that "one may disregard non-antagonistic contradictions [and] ignore them in politics. Life teaches us that even those contradictions which are not by their nature antagonistic may cause serious collisions if disregarded." He pointed out that "successes in socialist con-

---

[107] *Ibid.*

[108] *Ibid*, p. 8.

[109] *Ibid.*

struction" can be achieved only "when the policy of the ruling Communist Party rests on a sound scientific basis" and that "any underestimation of the role of Marxist-Leninist science and of its creative development, a narrow pragmatic interpretation of its tasks, disregard for the fundamental problems, the sway of expediency or scholastic theorizing are fraught with grave political and ideological consequences."[110] On this basis, he concluded that "we increasingly feel the need to do serious research into the political economy of socialism.... Marxism is not a dogma but an effective guide to action.... And to be able to keep pace with life, communists should carry forward and enrich the teaching of Marx in all directions, and creatively apply in practice his method of materialist dialectics.... Not the erosion of Marxist-Leninist teaching but, on the contrary, a struggle for its purity and creative development — such is the path to the cognition and solution of new problems."[111]

In their entirety, the views put forth by Yuri Andropov became the cornerstone of the policies which, after the CPSU's 1986 Congress, came to be known as "Restructuring" (*Perestroika*). Admittedly, while many of these views were not new and had been in circulation for some time, it was the first time that real practical steps were taken for their implementation. After all, Andropov's proposed reforms had originated with the 20th Congress (1956), where they should have been placed on the agenda, but were not. Unfortunately, many Party Congresses had come and gone with scant attention paid to these problems, allowing them to fester.

And thus, after a 25-year delay, the long-overdue reform of socialism's economic and political structures became the order of the day. Under Andropov's brief leadership, a serious campaign got underway to combat bureaucracy, corruption and economic parasitism that had gone unchecked, and had

---

[110] *Ibid*, p. 10.

[111] *Ibid*.

damaged the Party's prestige. The re-establishment of labor discipline and efficiency took the highest priority. Likewise, concerted efforts were made to combat loafing and idleness, while material incentives were strengthened and income equalization strategies were all but abandoned.

A systematic effort was undertaken for developing socialist democracy and further involvement of the masses in the political process. Some changes were made in the cadre training policies of the Party, etc. The combination of these measures to "correct" socialism and remove inefficiencies left a lasting impression of the Soviet people, giving them much ground for optimism. It seemed as if the Party had once again placed all its resources at the service of its historic mission and was well on its way to eliminate the conditions fueling the crisis.

Nonetheless, twenty-five years of delay in implementing the much-needed reform had badly strained the economic and political situation, creating many intractable problems for the Party. The matter was further complicated by the great technical advances in the imperialist countries — particularly in the area of computer technology and electronics — which had led in the military field to the gargantuan "Star Wars" program.

The mounting cost of military outlays coupled with misguided economic policies of the recent past had led to a much slower growth rate. Widespread dissatisfaction together with the West's anti-communist propaganda had left their mark on the masses, to a point where people were plainly dismayed at the status quo and the country's leadership. To these must also be added the troubling evolution of technocratic and bureaucratic layers that had grown within the Party and the State for almost three decades.

All these factors demanded the highest degree of alertness and vigilance on the part of the Party. Just as Yuri Andropov had stressed, the Party was called upon to fashion a policy based on the interests of the masses, with their participation, and on a solid scientific foundation. The Party had to achieve this while under direct or indirect propaganda offensive, subversion and distortions carried out by imperialist states and their intelligence services.

2. The 27th Congress: Boosting Socialism's Potential for Development

The 27th Congress of the CPSU which convened in 1986 — two years after Andropov's death — ratified a comprehensive package for the overhaul of the economic and political structures. The main slogan of the Congress was "Acceleration," and not the so-called "Openness" (*Glasnost*). The 12th Five Year Plan for 1986-1990 ratified at this Congress took up three themes: decentralization of the economic planning and modernization of production; establishment and boosting of material incentives; and, expansion of Socialist democracy.

The Congress also set out for itself the outlines of a 15-year plan for the 1986-2000 period in which provisions were made for an accelerated rate of growth at the close of the Century, after the completion of the 12th Five Year Plan. Some of the salient features of the plan for effecting sweeping changes in society were as follows:

- To speed up social and economic development
- To substantially accelerate scientific and technological progress
- To ensure a further rise in the well-being of all sections of the population and significant improvements in living conditions
- To raise per capita real income by 60-80%
- To accredit the social prestige of conscientious, high quality labor and professional skills
- With the growth of labor productivity, to increase

wages and improve the forms of payment; to provide greater moral encouragement to work collectives and individuals

• To improve working conditions; reduce the share of manual labor in production to 15-20% (from 45 percent)

• To satisfy more fully consumer demands for high quality and diversified goods

• To better the food supply to the level of scientifically substantiated norms for rational consumption

• To increase retail trade by 80%

• To develop a highly efficient service industry, to reduce the burden of housework

• To provide a flat or house for every family

• To double funds for social security, vacations, education and health services

• To encourage sports and other forms of recreation

• To persist in carrying out environmental protection work

• To double the national income, mainly by increasing labor productivity by 130-150%, toward achieving the world's highest level of social labor productivity

• To economize on materials and fuels, thereby meeting 75-80% of the increased requirements

• To raise the efficiency of capital investments, giving more emphasis to re-equipment and reconstruction rather than to building new enterprises from scratch

• To ensure the all-round acceleration of scientific and technological progress and general application of its results in industry and management, in the service sphere and everyday life

• To enhance the role of the Soviets of People's Deputies — the most important form of socialist government of the people — in economic, social and cultural development; to expand the working people's participation in administration.[112]

Pursuant to the goal of reducing the overcentralization

---

[112] Victor Perlo, *Super Profits and Crises: Modern U.S. Capitalism*, International Publishers, New York, 1988, pp. 509-510.

of the economy, many governmental functions were turned over to economic enterprises. The latter were empowered to make final decisions on matters related to the type and quantity of goods produced. The decision to purchase their raw material from a source of their choosing also fell under their purview. They were also given some limited autonomy on setting the wage levels for their employees as well as the prices of their products. Parallel to these trends, the prerogatives of economic enterprises were expanded. They were now expected to ensure their continued solvency and to regulate and fulfill their monthly planned quotas.

Next, in the sphere of material incentives, the policy of equalization of income levels was abandoned and, in fact, reversed. The abnormally low levels of income for occupations that required training, technical know-how and higher education came under sharp rebuke. Included in this category were medical doctors, teachers, engineers and scientists.

Some measures were also enacted to expand socialist democracy. For instance, enterprises and worker collectives were given a bigger say in determining the wages of employees on the basis of values created. During the 1986-1987 period, tens of thousands of factory and enterprise managers were at various times elected, promoted or even fired from their jobs through direct balloting by the workers. The question of workers' discipline was likewise delegated to shop floor representatives. They were even allowed to cut the wages and benefits of loafers and idlers.

Following up on these changes, the January 1987 Plenum of the CPSU Central Committee sharply criticized bureaucratism, particularly within the Party's own ranks, which finally set the stage for stemming the rise of bureaucracy through society.

Before long, the impact of these new changes was visible throughout the production sphere. Two years into the 12th Five Year Plan, the rise in the level of production in many sectors exceeded the objectives set down by the Plan. Of these, most striking was the housing sector in which the output rose to 2.3 million units in 1987, 15 percentage points above the projected figures![113]

At the June 25, 1987 Plenum, it was reported that:

> On the average, the rates in the increase of labor productivity during the past two years have increased, exceeding the mean annual figures of the Eleventh Five-Year Plan period in industry and construction by 30 percent, in agriculture by 100 percent and in railway transport by 200 percent....
>
> During 1985-1986, the average rate increases in industrial production amounted to 4.4 percent and in agriculture 3 percent....
>
> This year the rate increases in capital investments in social sphere are three times greater than in the national economy as a whole. [114]

All this was proof that the Party was able to regain the historical initiative in a short period of time if it reinstated scientific criteria in socialist production and implemented socialist democratic principles. It proved that a Party armed with Marxism-Leninism and powered by the creative energy of the working people could alleviate all obstacles, no matter how formidable, and to proceed to socialist renewal.

But, unfortunately, it was not just the Communists who were active players at the social level. A hiatus of 25 years in failing to implement the much-needed changes in the socialist system had brought about a tumor-like growth of a bureaucratic layer that was also very conscious of its own interests and who acted upon them; a layer that found its interest in obliterating socialism rather than redeeming it. It was this

---

[113] "Along the Road of Radical Reform," Statement by the State Committee of the USSR for Statistics On the Results of the Fulfillment of the USSR State Plan for Economic and Social Development in 1987, *Reprints from the Soviet Press*, March 1988, p. 44.

[114] *Reprints from the Soviet Press*, July 30/August 15, 1987, p. 6.

very layer, backed unconditionally by the international class enemies of the proletariat, that ultimately managed to turn the renewal process into one of dismantling and destroying socialism.

3. From Correction to Total Destruction — Gorbachev's "Humane Socialism" Model

While the 27th Congress could be considered a success in charting a new economic and political path for the Party and the working class, it was a setback of historic proportions with regard to the composition of the new leadership it elected. For it was here, at this Congress, that the growing bureaucratic and technocratic layers in the State apparatus seized the key strategic positions within the leadership of the Party and thus ensured their organizational dominance over its structures. While the 22nd Congress and its subsequent years constituted a turning point in which the growing layers of bureaucracy and technocracy secured their dominance over the Socialist State's political structures and institutions, the 27th Congress became another turning point in which these layers and their political representatives — in the body of Mikhail Gorbachev and his associates — over-ran and captured the high command of the proletariat's class power, i.e., the leadership of the Communist Party, and turned this power into an effective weapon for promoting their own interests through the destruction of socialism. Imperialism, which had long awaited this golden opportunity, also mobilized all material and propaganda resources at its disposal to assist this new faction within the Party leadership in its bid for the total domination of the CPSU.

Thus, the social and economic crisis that was brewing under the surface for three decades as a result of certain objective factors as well as subjective mistakes on the part of the Party, was now transformed into a full-fledged political crisis. From here on, the struggle for the correction of the past mistakes and renewal of socialism increasingly turned into a decisive struggle over the continued existence of the socialist system itself. The question of guaranteeing the survival of socialism, which from the very beginning had occupied the minds of the leaders of the revolution, including Lenin himself, once again took center stage, and the reality of class struggle under socialism, discounted for few decades, imposed itself on the Communists with all its weight.

In this way, two parallel but divergent currents emerged in the aftermath of the 27th Congress: one for the correction of Socialism's deficiencies and the acceleration of its growth based on the resolutions of the Congress, as supported by the working people and Communists; and the other for the destruction of socialism and steering the course of events in the direction of the interests of the bureaucratic and techno-cratic layers who had seized power in the 27th Congress, and who enjoyed imperialism's unqualified support. While Communists insisted on strengthening socialist principles and laws within the economy and expanding socialist democracy at the social level, Gorbachev and his company, under the guise of the so-called "new thinking," tried to move the events in the direction of implementing rapid changes in Socialism's political structure and imposing bourgeois de-mocracy and free-market economy on Soviet society.

In the years immediately following the 27th Congress, when this faction's hold on power was still tenuous, it acted with great prudence: while busily consolidating itself within the high echelons of Party leadership and assigning every important post to its loyal supporters, it purported to stand for the "acceleration" of Socialist development. During the years 1987-89, it deployed every organizational means possi-ble to undermine the Communists within the leadership of the Party and change the course of developments. One after the other, the plenary meetings of the Central Committee

159

held after the 27th Congress made decisions that were solely within the jurisdiction of the Party congresses. The process of purging "conservatives," i.e., Communists who acted as an obstacle to the faction's intended reforms, from the leading organs of the Party — almost always conducted through a campaign of lies and vilification — took an increasing proportion each passing day. Each illegal purge of Communists from the Party leadership was loudly applauded and cheered on by the propaganda services of the imperialist countries, providing the newly-fanged "democrats" within the Communist Party additional recognition and "legitimacy."

Alongside this, the authority to make crucial decisions bearing on the fate of the nation as a whole was preemptively removed from the Central Committee and increasingly transferred to the newly-formed bureaucratic structures, constantly diminishing the Party's supervision over the state's affairs. Concurrent with the reduction of the role of the Party, the central planning system was also dismantled rapidly. The number of government personnel involved in the administration of the economy was cut from 200,000 in 1987 to 58,000 in 1989.[115] This was at the time when, by comparison, the U.S. Departments of Treasury, Commerce and Agriculture, whose role in the U.S. capitalist economy is far less than those in the Soviet Union, had 300,000 employees in the same years.[116]

With the growing organizational muscle of this faction, its true political line also became more apparent and increasingly imposed on society. As the faction's power consolidated, its ideological and political attacks on so-called "barracks socialism," on planned economy, and on anti-reform "conservatives" intensified. In the name of combating "Stalinism," the faction's representatives used the mass media to wage a

---

[115] Victor Perlo, "The Economic and Political Crisis in the USSR," *Political Affairs,* August 1991, p. 14.

[116] *Ibid.*

frontal attack against the whole history and the achievements of Socialism, against the CPSU and the Socialist way of life, and against such important principles as democratic centralism which for them signified "lack of democracy."

Increasingly, Gorbachev himself took aim at the past achievements of socialism. His repeated charge that central planning and the Socialist system have been the main cause of economic stagnation stirred much doubt and disillusionment toward Socialism. This was at the time when even the Western pundits and reporters had to concede that despite the slowdown of economic activity, the real income of the Soviet people had registered an average growth rate of 3.47 percent over the 1960-1984 period, which translated into a tripling of the living standards for this period.[117] According to Nikolai Ryzhkov, one of Gorbachev's closest associates, in the 35 years preceding 1987, the national income of the Soviet Union had grown 6.5 times, a figure which amounts to an average annual growth rate of 5.5 percent. (During the same period, the U.S. national income had risen 2.8 times — an average annual growth rate of 3 percent — yet no one dared to call it economic stagnation!)[118]

In its effort to prepare the political atmosphere for the introduction of free market economy, this faction began to counterpose the New Economic Policy (NEP) to the Socialist system of central planning of the economy, insisting that the abandonment of the NEP was the first historical step in violation of Socialist principles. Step by step, calls for implementation of political reforms "from above" and establishment of Western-style "democracy" replaced the policy of economic reforms in favor of the working people. It was increasingly argued that without such political reforms from above, no economic reform from below would be possible.

Needless to say, up to this point, the political representa-

---

[117] *Ibid., p. 12.*

[118] *Ibid.*

tives of this faction did their best to hide their policies as steps toward safeguarding the Socialist essence of the system. The concept of "market economy" was invariably cast as a benign and harmless concept. Even the staunchest defenders of capitalism and anti-communist supporters of this faction were careful not to be seen using the word "capitalism" in public, preferring instead to pay lip-service to workers' demands. But all this changed in the latter months of 1988, after this faction succeeded in imposing its policy of "new thinking," "openness" and "democracy" on the leadership of the Party in the 19th All Union Conference of the CPSU held on June 30, 1988. From this point on, the main slogan of the 27th Congress of the CPSU, namely, the "acceleration" of socialist development, was completely abandoned in favor of the narrow interests of these layers.

With its power firmly in place, and its platform forced upon the Party as a whole, the faction launched an open and sweeping ideological, political and economic attack on socialism. "New Thinking," which was at first beguilingly peddled as the "expansion of socialism," was now openly used as a lightning rod for the restoration of capitalist relations in the USSR. Circles close to this faction waged a vicious campaign against the basic principles of Socialism and Marxism-Leninism. The well-known leaders of this faction, like Foreign Minister Eduard Shevardnadze and intellectuals like Stanislav Menshikov, essentially used the concept of "new thinking" as a fig leaf for justifying and openly promoting capitalism and defending imperialism's foreign policy. During 1989-90, Gavril Popov, who was assigned by the faction as the editor of the CPSU's *Economic Affairs* journal, used the pages of that journal as a tribune for attacking Marx's theory of surplus value, claiming that capitalists incurred their profits not from the exploitation of workers, but from their "mental labor"! In other articles, they attacked Lenin's theory of imperialism claiming that big capitalist powers were not responsible for the plunder of other countries! The reality of class struggle and the contradiction between labor and capital were increasingly negated while calls were consistently made for "de-ideologization" of relations between socialist and imperialist states. The mass media were filled with prescriptions by prominent Western capitalists for "reforming" the economic and the political structure of socialism. Invitations were readily extended to many such unsavory figures, especially "experts" and "economists" affiliated with Harvard University's Department of Soviet Studies, to teach "modern economics" to the Soviet intelligentsia. And, most shocking of all, all these anti-Communist propaganda campaigns were conducted in the name of the leadership of the CPSU!

Gus Hall, Chairman of the Communist Party, USA, provided a vivid description of the anti-socialist ideological offensive that was underway at that time:

> If you put together the lack of ideological education and the fact that during the past five years there has been no defense of socialism, you get the picture of how lopsided the ideological struggle has been. The seven newspapers that advocated socialism have been silenced. The mass media is open to every anti-socialist outfit from around the world. Radio Free Europe and Radio Liberty have their offices in all the big cities and daily access to the airwaves. Every right-wing U.S. TV preacher is on the air in the big cities in the Soviet Union. CIA-sponsored organizations, including the ultra-right Heritage foundation, have programs that air throughout the Soviet Union. John Sununu, heads of FBI departments and leaders of the Young Republicans regularly lectured to the staffs of the Central Committee and the Komsomol. The U.S. Army has sent instructors to lecture the Soviet Union on "making their military more democratic." U.S. advisers, economists, ideologues and professors are active adherents of capitalist economy and bourgeois democracy in every institute and every level of government. And of course, there are more student exchange programs, where Soviet men and women spend years at Harvard and Yale learning to become "entrepreneurs."

163

While the Soviet Union has opened the floodgates for every foreign magazine and newspaper, including pornographic and sensational garbage, they have cancelled every foreign Communist newspaper. This extensive ideological penetration has been going on with the approval of Gorbachev and the circle around him. [119]

This all-out ideological attack on Socialism was combined with the gradual but conscious dismantling of socialist relations of production, their substitution with capitalist relations, and attempts for the creation of a new capitalist class in the country. In 1990, Mikhail Gorbachev himself officially announced the abandonment of the fundamental principles of socialism, i.e., public ownership of the means of production, planned economy and other socialist provisions of the Constitution of the USSR. He publicly declared that the "former theoretical and practical model of socialism, which was imposed on the party for decades, has proved to be untenable.... Our aim is to create a mixed, multiform economy, in which all forms of property ownership develop freely ... in order to give the biggest number of working people the opportunity to become owners...."[120]

This, however, was just a fig leaf. Changes went far beyond a mere "diversity of forms of ownership." In reality, promoting private ownership and privatization of state enterprises became the faction's highest order of priority. This policy reflected itself in the February 1990 documents of the Central Committee of the CPSU in the following words: "Another important task is the transformation of state property into one of these privately owned 'modern forms.'"[121] Gorbachev gave the following ideological justification for the sharp turn in

---

[119] Gus Hall, "The Crisis in the Soviet Union," Remarks to the Special Meeting of the National Committee, Communist Party, U.S.A., September 8, 1991, p. 3.

[120] *Ibid.*, p. 6.

[121] Victor Perlo, "The Economic and Political Crisis in the USSR," *Political Affairs,* August 1991, p. 13.

government policy: "The most important feature of this draft is a resolute rupture with the obsolete ideological dogmas and stereotypes and the striving to bring our world outlook and policy in line...."[122] Thus the public ownership of the means of production was declared as "obsolete ideological dogma," and private property became a "modern form" of ownership in the Soviet Union.

This official declaration of policy of privatization, which was nothing less than a declaration of victory of a pro-capitalist coup from the above, did not reflect the wishes of 19 million card-carrying Party members. Rather, it was the demand of the "majority" of a Central Committee which had already been purged of its "conservative" Communist members. Moreover, this resolution was in clear violation of the Constitution of the USSR which stipulated in no uncertain terms that "Major matters of the state shall be submitted to nationwide discussion and put to a popular vote (referendum)."[123]

Naturally, a transition from socialism to capitalism could not be legal without the consent of the Soviet people. But the organizers of the pro-capitalist coup could care less for the wishes of the people. They not only ignored the 1990 referendum in which 76 percent of the Soviet people had voted for maintaining the USSR, but never carried out a second referendum on the private ownership of land. They were fully aware that in this referendum, too, they would be completely defeated.

Toward the end of 1990, ignoring the wishes of millions of Communists and the working people, Gorbachev and his co-conspirators officially passed laws for the privatization of public enterprises and the establishment of the stock exchange.

---

[122] Gus Hall, *op. cit.*, p. 6.

[123] *Constitution (Fundamental Law) of the Union of Soviet Socialist Republics,* adopted at the Seventh (Special) Session of the Supreme Soviet of the USSR, Ninth Convention, October 7, 1977. Novosti Press Agency Publishing House, Moscow, 1977, Article 5, p. 20.

They hastily turned over the ownership of these enterprises to the same bureaucratic layers that managed them. With people's national wealth thus auctioned off to this layer, yesterday's managers were transformed into instant capitalists, and the capitalist coup expanded from the political sphere into the economic sphere. The plunder of public property and its private appropriation by the state's bureaucratic layers became the established norm in the economy. Mafia-like layers of newly-emerged capitalists grew like mushrooms, accumulating wealth of astronomical proportions on the backs of the working people. Such imperialist financial institutions as Merril Lynch were enlisted by Gorbachev and his associates to supervise and direct the process of privatization of state enterprises, thus becoming the imperialist guardians of the Soviet economy.

Another step taken by the coup leaders was the imposition of capitalist relations on the distribution of consumer goods. In the name of "improving the quality and quantity of goods and services," they moved to create the so-called "producers' cooperatives," which, contrary to Soviet law, did not exclusively rely on the labor of their own members. In many major cities and republics, authorities belonging to this faction openly ignored the laws in forming these phony "cooperatives." In less than a year, by the end of 1989, these so-called "producers' cooperatives" had more than five million workers in their employment. On the other hand, the real cooperatives were undermined to a point where, by 1991, their number shrank to 20 percent of all cooperatives in the country.[124] As a result of these policies, the distribution of basic commodities needed by the working people was shifted from genuine cooperatives and public stores to the newly-formed capitalist "cooperatives," where the prices were prohibitively high and, in most cases, sales were made in foreign currencies. All this

---

[124] Victor Perlo, "The Economic and Political Crisis in the USSR," *Political Affairs,* August 1991, p. 14.

was going on at the time when Gorbachev was deceitfully assuring workers that the "collective ownership" of cooperatives and private companies would not only "strengthen the democratic pillars society" but would also turn the workers into the "masters of the means of production," a path in which, according to Gorbachev, "there is no basis for exploitation."[125]

The cumulative effect of these treacherous policies was a sharp decline in the level of production, leading to severe shortages of basic commodities for the working people. Along with the intensification of production crisis, Gorbachev and his administration reneged on their earlier commitment to the scientific-technological development of the economy. The funds for investment in capital goods production were cut drastically and the budget for research and development in the civilian sector of the economy was reduced by four billion rubles.[126] Instead, the attention was focused on investments in the consumer-goods sector in order to fill in the bottlenecks caused by the black market and the capitalists' outright sabotages. But, as expected, these investments, too, were lost in the bottomless pockets of the private sector.

To compensate for the shortages of basic necessities, the coup leaders increasingly turned to imports of consumer goods, thus throwing the economy's gates wide open to the flood of goods from Western countries. This open-door import policy led to alarmingly high levels of foreign debts and an increasing dependence on international capitalist banks and financial institutions. According to Western estimates, by 1990, the Soviet Unions's foreign debt, which was intentionally kept low throughout Soviet history, quickly rose to the astronomical figure of $58-69 billion.[127] Thus, the coun-

---

[125] *Ibid.*

[126] *Ibid.*, p. 16.

[127] *Ibid.*

try's creditworthiness took a nose-dive.

In 1990, for the first time in Soviet history, the country's Gross National Product (GNP), its national income, and labor productivity took a downturn, and by mid-1991 this downward trend assumed catastrophic proportions. According to the State Statistical Office of the USSR, "compared to 1990 figures, in the first half of 1991 the GNP has declined by 10 percent, national income by 12 percent, and social labor productivity by 11 percent. The decline in industrial production continues in all branches and has reached six percent compared to last year.... The chemical and timber industry has declined by 50 percent, metallurgy by 46 percent, energy production by 34 percent, and the machine industry by 37 percent. Coal production has decreased 41 million tons and oil production has decreased by six percent."[128] On the other hand, in the same year, the inflation rate rose to 100 percent and it was reported by various sources that 60 percent of Soviet workers lived on or under the poverty line. All this caused much suffering among the people, aggravating an already volatile situation.

Along with people's increasing problems and their declining standard of living, the beast of national enmity that Soviet achievements has succeeded in vanquishing for the past 70 years, rose its ugly head once again. National conflicts and military confrontations between various nationalities — some of which were consciously stirred up by the coup leaders and imperialist forces — on the one hand, and the growing discontent among the people and their increasing protest against the situation caused by government policies, on the other, intensified the political crisis within the country. As a result, the danger of the disintegration of the USSR was thus added to the problems already caused by Gorbachev's "new thinking."

---

[128] Translated from *Nameh Mardom*, organ of the Tudeh Party of Iran, No. 357, September 3, 1991, p. 4.

The pro-capitalist coup leaders used the growing mass discontent, which they had consciously helped create, to deal the final blow against Socialism. Having succeeded in staging an organizational coup within the Party, followed by an economic coup at the social level, they moved to stage yet another political coup at the government level with plans to dismember the Soviet state. First, the Baltic republics seceded from the Soviet Union and then, in September 1990, Yeltsin announced the withdrawal of the Russian Republic from the USSR. Following Russia, Ukraine, Belorussia and Kazakhstan declared their decision to secede from the Soviet Union. Then, following the abortive August 1991 events, the CPSU itself was declared "illegal" by Yeltsin; all its assets and properties were confiscated, and the persecution and arrest of Party members began throughout the country. Finally, with the illegal break-up of the USSR in 1992, the coup leaders achieved their ultimate political objective.

In this manner, the process which had originally begun to accelerate the development of socialism, was transformed into a process of dismantlin of socialism from the above, and the ultimate destruction of the Socialist state in the USSR. As Gus Hall has explained,

> It was about two years into perestrika that I became concerned not with the specifics but with the general direction of the process. Along with it, old structures were dismantled with nothing to take their place. Decentralization was carried to an extreme. Factories and industrial complexes were left in a vacuum, without plans, and more important, with no links with each other.
>
> In the first year, thousands of factories closed their doors. The old economic structure, with all its weaknesses, was the basis on which the Soviet Union increased production every year. This structure was dismantled, including the links between industries and agriculture, as well as a centrally controlled and coordinated transportation system.... The dismantling of the existing system caused chaos and great disturbances of the economy.

169

Every year since perestroika was sidetracked, production continued to decline.... The policies implemented under Gorbachev's leadership created havoc in the Soviet economy. It went off the socialist rails. The pro-capitalist, anti-socialist policies and propaganda of the right wing forces did serious ideological damage. Ideology went off the Communist, Marxist-Leninist rails. These mistakes, miscalculations and wrong policies were the result of human error.

In the Soviet Union, the correction of mistakes and debates around theory got out of control. The anti-socialist elements were able to gain the upper hand. For a period of five years no one defended socialism — its history and achievements, its right to defend itself and preserve the socialist system. The slander and vilification of socialist system and the Communist Party went mainly unanswered. This led to mass confusion. The corrupt, the anti-Communists and the criminals got into positions of power. They took over the mass media. The Communist Party of the Soviet Union went into a tailspin, from which it is yet to extricate itself."[129]

And all this, one might add, was a direct result of the takeover of the Party by bureaucratic and technocratic layers within the state.

[129] Gus Hall, "The Crisis in the Soviet Union," *Remarks to the Special Meeting of the National Committee, Communist Party, USA.*, September 8, 1991, p. 6

Conclusions:

Was the Collapse Inevitable?

The fact that the conscious shift toward the destruction of socialism was never the wish of the working class and people of the Soviet Union is beyond dispute. The proof lies not only in the 1990 referendum in which the great majority of the Soviet people voted in favor of maintaining the Soviet Union, but also in the fact that all these developments were initiated from the above and within the leadership of the CPSU itself. Throughout this period, one is hard pressed to find an instance of mass demonstration or organized social movement by the people aimed against the socialist order, against the Socialist state, or against the Communist Party itself. No pressure from below can be said to have been responsible for the dismantling of socialist rule in the USSR.

On the other hand, the fact that the vast majority of Party members were against these developments is also well-documented and beyond dispute. This sentiment was reflected especially in the 28th Congress of the CPSU, held in July 1990, where the leadership was severely taken to task for its policies. Nevertheless, despite all opposition from the delegates, the coup leaders managed to advance their objectives in the 28th Congress. Igor Lygachev, member of CPSU Political Bureau and Secretary of the Central Committee, whose principled stand against Gorbachev's policies cost him his position later on in 1990, explained in the "Constitutional Court," held for his and other Party leaders' "trial," how

171

Gorbachev and his associates concealed their true intentions, and even decisions, from the Central Committee and the CPSU as a whole:

> ... the demands of Party organizations in Moscow, Leningrad, Kiev and others, as well as my own memos to the Political Bureau about the need for convening an extraordinary session of the Central Committee to discuss the issues of Party unity and the country's integrity, were concealed from the Central Committee.... During the years 1990-91, the CPSU was left out of the decision making process on important issues, including such critical ones as the transition to market economy and privatization of ownership. These issues were brought to the attention of the Central Committee only after they had been decided upon.... I feel guilty for not having used everything at my disposal to prevent this transformation in the country's policy.... [130]

Lygachev resolutely rejected the claim by "new thinkers" that Communists were responsible for the destruction of the socialist order:

> The claim made in the Court by the President's representatives that "the economic order was ruined by the Party leadership" is a lie through and through. It is an attempt by the democrats to blame the Communists for the destructive work of the government.
>
> Statistics demonstrate that during the post-war period, the country's industrial production increased 24 times and the national income rose 16 times. I remember very clearly that during the early years of *Perestrioka* (1985-1989), the level of production in industry and agriculture reached its highest level. Housing construction also showed similar growth.
>
> During those years, people enjoyed their highest standard of living. Things were improving because society's renewal was being carried out on the basis of socialism and within

---

[130] Translated from *Nameh Mardom*, No. 388, 19 Aban 1371 (November 10, 1992), p. 7.

the framework of the Soviet system.

Then, the restructuring process lost its socialist and democratic direction and the course of returning to a bourgeois
order was adopted. "New thinkers" and democrats are
the ones who created the present conditions for the country.[131]

Historical facts also bear out Lygachev's contentions. The
loss of the socialist state had nothing to do with the past
economic problems of the Soviet Union. The CPSU, albeit
with delay, had set forth in 1982 the proper and necessary
measures for the rapid elimination of objective conditions
that had led to the crisis, and had in fact made important
strides toward that end. The positive effects of these measures
were increasingly visible in all spheres of social life, and society
had taken significant steps in the direction of overcoming
the deficiencies. What turned this process of correction into
a process of dismantling, and the ultimate destruction of the
socialist order, was the conspiratorial actions of a specific
social strata which, thanks to the past mistakes and neglects
of the Party leadership, had grown in its size and strength.
This strata, through time, managed to seize the Party leadership, and took advantage of the tremendous material and
propaganda support it received from imperialism to stage a
capitalist coup from above.

That is why today, with many historical facts uncovered,
one can categorically state that the causes of the destruction
of the socialist state in the Soviet Union were basically unrelated to the objective conditions that had given rise to the
crisis in socialism. The destruction of the socialist state was
not a consequence of the development of antagonistic and
irreconcilable contradictions within the socialist system. Nor
was it a result of the take-over of the socialist state by a
so-called "new ruling class" — e.g., bureaucracy, etc. — as
some have claimed; or the transformation of the nature of

---

[131] *Ibid.*, pp. 6-7.

the socialist system as a whole into some other system — such as "state capitalism," etc. — as some others have claimed. Rather, it was a result of conscious acts of sabotage carried out by a certain faction within the leadership of the Party — a faction whose narrow interests coincided with those of capitalists and imperialists, and who greatly benefited from the unconditional support of the imperialist states in its efforts to undermine socialism in the USSR.

Nonetheless, it was not a foregone conclusion that this anti-working-class, anti-Socialist plot should have prevailed. A timely and vigilant move by the Communists, through a mass mobilization of millions of pro-Socialist workers, could have foiled the plot and averted the tragedy. This conclusion, however, raises a whole host of questions that beg for answers, including: Why did the Soviet working class, whose objective class interests were directly threatened by these developments, fail to take an active role in defense of socialism? And, why did the Party and the majority of Communists fail to expose this plot in time and put up an effective resistance against it?

The Role of "New Thinking"

One of the prime factors contributing to indecisiveness on the part of Communists and the working people was the phenomenon of "new thinking." The backdrop for the emergence of this phenomenon was the set of corrective measures initiated by the CPSU itself to alleviate the existing deficiencies of the socialist system. For this reason, the true essence of "new thinking" was obscured in the eyes of the working masses and Communists for a long time. This is especially true about the anti-working class aspects of this phenomenon, which were injected into the movement step-by-step and in a piecemeal way and, therefore, their immediate effects were kept imperceptible for the masses.

At the same time, the fact that such views were being articulated by the Party leadership itself, played a significant role in obfuscating the true essence of this phenomenon and disarming the masses against it. Ever since the October Revolution, the Soviet people had known and trusted only one Party — the CPSU — and its leadership. The fact that the pro-capitalist coup was carried out in the name of the great Party of Lenin was the prime reason for people's confusion and lack of resistance. The people of Soviet Union accepted the changes on the basis of their historical trust in the CPSU, and it was only after disaster had struck that they realized the true meaning of these changes.

In this connection, the deceitful actions of Gorbachev and his associates played a key role in confusing and disarming the masses. While covertly carrying out an anti-Socialist plot, they publicly posed as champions of socialist progress, claiming that these changes would guarantee "more socialism" for the working people. One cannot doubt for a moment that the masses of workers and the people of Soviet Union would have reacted differently had they known at the outset the true essence of "new thinking" and the "new thinkers'" plan for dismantling Socialism in the USSR.

The objective ramifications of the "new thinkers'" economic policies also played a significant role in creating apathy among the working people. The unprecedented rise in poverty and unemployment, galloping inflation and the drastic drop in the value of the ruble, which had cut deeply into the purchasing power of the working people, forcing them into hunger and destitution, caused great disaffection among the people; and since all these disastrous changes were made in the name of the Party, the working people began to blame the Party and the socialist state for their deteriorating conditions. While the initial policies aimed at accelerating socialist growth had heartened the masses of people, the deviations from these policies and the headlong descent toward capitalism served to disillusion the people and turn them away from the Party and its leadership.

At the same time, the ensuing shortages and the mounting

poverty among the masses had the added consequence of turning workers' attention away from the political process and pulling them towards eking out a meager existence for themselves and their families. This was another important cause of people's lack of response to social and political issues. This phenomenon vividly demonstrated the veracity of Marx's observation that: "... the first premise of all human existence and, therefore, all history... [is] that men must be in a position to live in order to be able to 'make history'.... The first historical act is thus ... the production of material life itself."[132]

In this manner, "new thinking" and the political and economic policies ensuing from it not only caused confusion among the masses of working people and kept them from taking a firm political stand against proponents of capitalism, but created the material conditions for the success of a pro-capitalist coup by threatening the very livelihood of the masses and thus driving them away from the political process. In other words, "new thinking" acted as a doubled-edged sword in the hands of the enemies of the working class: On the one hand, it caused confusion in the people's minds about the true meaning of developments in their society; and on the other hand, it undermined people's political resistance by deteriorating their living conditions to a point where economic survival became their main concern of the day. The secret of the success of the pro-capitalist coup leaders lies in their effective use of this double-edged sword.

Lack of Resolute Response by the Communists

If one can attribute the masses' lack of response to their confusion and deteriorating living conditions, such a reasoning

---

[132] *The German Ideology*, International Publishers, New York, 1947, p. 48; *MECW*, Vol. 5, pp.41-2.

cannot be used to explain the lack of resolute response by the Communists. For, if the masses could be said to be theoretically or ideologically ill-equipped to understand the true essence of "new thinking," Communists had no dearth of knowledge to identify that devious phenomenon for what it was. Should they have known from the outset that "new thinking" and its premises was totally alien to the teachings of Marxism-Leninism and communism? Should they have recognized that it represented the outlook and interests of the state bureaucracy? Negation of the reality of class struggle, negation of the proletarian hegemony over the political structures of socialism, rejection of the working class power and a non-class approach to the concept of democracy, rejection of the concept of a class-based, ideological state, calls for "de-ideologization" of international relations between socialist and capitalist states, rejection of proletarian internationalism, rejection of the concept of imperialism and emphasis on the "convergence" of the socialist and capitalist systems, and most importantly, open rejection of socialist ownership of the means of production as the most fundamental principle of socialism — all were in direct contradiction to the ideological and theoretical foundations of the Marxist-Leninist worldview.

But despite all blatant deviations of the proponents of "new thinking," Soviet communists did not put up a meaningful resistance, and as Igor Lygachev said, failed to "mobilize their resources" to expose the plot, alert the masses to the incipient danger, and call them into action. A timely and resolute rejection of these deviations by the Communists could have averted the disaster. But, unfortunately, it did not materialize, and the enemies of the working class and socialism took full advantage of the Communists' hesitation to further confuse the masses and deliver their decisive blow against socialism in the USSR.

Although the underlying reasons for the Soviet Communists' lack of vigilance and resolute response against "new thinking" and its deviant policies are yet to be fully analyzed, certain factors can be identified on the basis of the more general historical trends:

1. Throughout this period, the Communists seem to have acted on the basis of the false historical premise that "the process of construction of socialism has reached a point where it has become irreversible." Over-estimation of the potentials, capabilities and great achievements of socialism, on the one hand, and under-estimation of the destructive capabilities of the enemies of socialism, especially those of the imperialist states, on the other hand, had a combined effect of blinding them to the true dangers that threatened the very existence of the socialist system.

2. The concept of the "Party of the Entire People," which had dominated the CPSU's outlook and its cadre policy for the past several decades, not only had dulled the ideological vigilance within the Party ranks, but had also flung its doors wide open to the penetration of non-proletarian elements, thus weakening the Communists' relative strength in face of the non-proletarian tendencies within the Party. As a result, these elements increasingly influenced the internal decision-making processes of the Party, thus hindering the emergence of a coherent and solid resistance to the Party leadership's ideological and political deviations.

3. The task of marshalling the development toward "acceleration" of socialist growth, which was originally predicated on broad participation of the working people throughout society, was, in practice, gradually shifted into the hands of the Party intellectuals and technocrats whose approach to these developments was less class-based and ideological and more politically-motivated and pragmatic. Not only did they fail to understand the importance of working class participation in this process, but by confining all decision-making to the exclusive domain of high-level Party leadership, they effectively cut off workers from participation in the restructuring process. This not only weakened the Communists'

position in this process, but also led to the adoption of certain subjectivist and accommodationist policies that further paved the way for the ultimate domination of "new thinking" over Party policies.

4. Political pragmatism within the world Communist movement, which had made a taboo out of any form of open criticism of the Communist Parties and socialist states, again pushed many world Communist and workers parties into a passive silence in face of the destructive policies carried out by the leadership of the CPSU. While a good deal of this silence derived from the confounding effects of "new thinking" itself, one cannot doubt that the traditional norms governing inter-Party relations on the world level played an important role in the initial silence of many of these parties. Experience shows that, with the exception of a few parties, most Communist and workers parties around the world used the refrain "the Soviet comrades are in the thick of struggle and know best" to avoid having to take an explicit position against these deviations. They started to take open positions only after a part of the CPSU leadership had already declared its opposition to these policies. But it was too little, too late; and the opportunity for forestalling the capitalist coup had already passed.

It seems that all these factors, as well as many other historical causes that need further study, have contributed to the Communists' indecision and lack of timely response to the destructive policies that transformed the process of Socialist renewal into a process of destruction of socialism in the USSR and other socialist countries. But this by no means implies an under-estimation of the heroic struggles of the Communists, and especially Soviet and other socialist bloc Communists, in defense of socialism and of Communist principles. The very fact that the success of a pro-capitalist coup in the land of Soviets could be secured only through banning the CPSU, confiscation of Party assets, arrest and persecution of Communists throughout the country, and bombing the country's Parliament, is a glaring and undeniable testimony to the heroic role that the the CPSU and the Soviet Communists played in defense of socialism and its great achievements. Neither the destruction of the socialist states nor any historical setback can negate the value of their struggles and the tremendous achievements of Communists for the working people of the socialist counties and the world during the past 80 years.

The Future

Today, following the dismantling of the socialist states in the USSR and other eastern European countries, there are those who want us to believe that the October Revolution has come to an end; that "Communism is dead;" that Marxism-Leninism has met its doom; that the working class has lost its revolutionary potential; that the class struggle is no more; and that imperialism has relinquished its exploitation and oppression of the masses around the world. They urge the Communists to abandon their scientific-revolutionary ideology and jump on the band wagon of social democracy, bourgeois democracy and, ultimately, opportunism and nihilism, if they don't want to be "discarded" by history.

But a simple glance at the saddening fate of those who turned such imperialist propaganda into their battlecry proves the absurdity of these claims. Less than a decade after the dismantling of the socialist states, it has become quite clear who are being discarded by history: not Communists and Marxist-Leninists — who have been steadily regaining their strength — but the very people who turned their backs on the working class, Communist ideology, the October revolution and socialism. All we need to do is ask: where has history placed the likes of Gorbachev, Yakovlev, Shevardnadze and Yeltsin? In the historical context, a decade is a very short time. But that was all it took for history to pass its judgment on those who betrayed socialism and turned their backs on the future of humankind.

Indeed, historical reality is rapidly re-imposing itself upon the minds of the masses throughout the world. The working people, especially those living in the former socialist countries, are rapidly realizing the true nature of the raw deal they received from imperialism and its quasi-Communist allies. The recent turn of events in Lithuania, Slovenia, Tajikstan, Hungary, Bulgaria and, most importantly, in the Russian Republic, has once again demonstrated the fact that the forward march of history cannot be reversed; and that those who commit the mistake of making such an attempt are promptly and most severely punished by human history itself.

The fact is, the process that began with the Great October Socialist Revolution was rooted in a historical necessity; it was a response to certain objective needs of the human society at a certain level of its historical development. These objective historical needs have not been, *and cannot be*, answered by capitalism, and for this very reason, one cannot doubt for a moment that the October Revolution, the struggle for socialism and Communism, continues.

At the same time, it is undeniable that the recent setback in the course of human progress has led to temporary, yet important, shifts in the relative balance of international class forces and, as a result, in the minds of many human beings. Just as in the past eighty years, the powerful magnet of the growing socialism had attracted a significant segment of the middle strata and especially the progressive intelligensia to the cause of socialism and Communism, today the setback in the process of socialist construction and the temporary global sway of imperialism has once again turned capitalism into a powerful gravitational force for these very strata. This new tendency, which is based more than anything else on a sense of defeat and powerlessness in the face of imperialism, has a right-oriented, social-democratic, and in many instances opportunistic nature. It rejects such concepts as class struggle,

181

imperialism and internationalism and the necessity of ending capitalist exploitation. This tendency, which tries to limit the struggles of the working people to a mere defense of bourgeois democracy and the "reforming" of capitalism, now advocates the "dissolution" of Communist Parties or their transformation into social democratic ones. Hiding behind a "Marxist" mask, it tries to reject Leninism and the working people's struggles of the past eighty years. But rejecting Leninism is rejecting Marxism; and that is why today, a steadfast ideological struggle against such opportunistic tendencies constitutes an integral part of the Communists' fight against capitalism's all-out war against socialism.

The class struggle for socialism continues. But the victory in this struggle hinges upon the re-organization of a broad, international Communist-workingclass-anti-imperialist united front to defend the existing socialist countries, protect the legal activity of all Communist and working class parties; safeguard the past achievements of the Communist and working class movements in both capitalist and former socialist countries, and support the anti-imperialist and national liberation struggles of the working people in underdeveloped countries. Only thus can the international Communist and working class movement overcome the present setback and lead the billions of exploited and oppressed working people across the world toward their final emancipation from class exploitation and oppression.

Afterword

The conscious process of building Communism is historically undertaken by men and women who, regardless of how much they may have mentally surpassed the theoretical and ideological boundaries of the capitalist system, are nonetheless the children of the old order and, therefore, carry on their backs all of its onerous load. Unlike Hegel's "Absolute Spirit," they have not entered history from its finishing point, but are themselves created by, and act within the limits set by, this history. They, like the society they live in, carry the heavy load of the past on their shoulders — a load which hinders and limits their movements. Parting with this heavy load cannot be the work of one or two generations. It can be done only thought the long and protracted struggle of progressive humanity for building a Communist society. In this vein, the process of building socialism and Communism is at the same time the process of education and evolution of all living human beings who struggle for this goal.

The subjective vision of these human beings of a socialist society, perfect as it may seem in their minds, loses its perfection as soon as it enters the objective realm of history. The primacy of consciousness and the subjective element in the process of construction of socialism by no means implies an unconditional surrender of objective reality to the wishes of the vanguards of human progress. The only difference between this and the past processes, as Marx has emphasized, is that here, for the first time in history, it is the living present that rules over the dead past. But even here, the rule of the living present is not an absolute, unconditional rule. The legacy of the past always imposes itself upon the present. To escape this legacy, to circumscribe it, can be done only

183

through a better understanding of the laws that govern objective reality and through conforming with the requirements of these laws. Man learned to fly only after he adequately understood the laws of gravity. The steady march toward Communism similarly requires a full understanding of objective laws and devising proper means to harness them. And in this process, anytime, anywhere, that human consciousness and subjectivity come into conflict — and not conformity — with these objective laws and requirements, the ground is paved once again for the rule of the dead past over the living present. In the deepest philosophical sense, this has been the ultimate cause of the crisis in socialism.

At the same time, it would be a grave mistake to forget that the Communists' subjective errors, regardless of how grave and critical they may have been, occurred within the framework of an extremely difficult and unequal struggle against world imperialism and its intrigues; that they have occurred in the course of traversing a completely uncharted historical path for which there does not exist any pre-established guidelines. Thus, the point here is not to blame these true vanguards of human progress for their errors and missteps in the course of their noble struggle. Rather, it is to learn from their positive and negative experiences in order to avoid similar errors in our long-drawn struggle for the liberation of humankind from exploitation and oppression.

Communists, as the vanguard of human liberation, have no choice but to learn from the past in their continued struggle for socialism and Communism. They are fully aware that in their difficult struggle, they are bound to face other, similarly difficult, obstacles; that they could be struck down again and again; and that they may feel the bitter taste of more setbacks along the way. But they are also equally aware that, as in the past, they shall overcome all obstacles; they shall rise once again; and they shall continue to add to the roster of their great achievements. As Lenin emphasized after the victory of the October Revolution:

We have made a start. When, at what date and time, and the proletarians of which nation will complete this process is not important. The important thing is that the ice has been broken; the road is open, the way has been shown.[133]

---

[133] Speech on the Fourth Anniversary of the October Revolution, *Collected Works*, English edition, Vol. 33, p. 57.

Index

Andropov, Yuri, 147-54,
    155 passim
Brezhnev, Leonid, 457 124, 147
Brzezinski, Zbignew, 44
Bukharin, N.I. 87, 88
CPSU, 13, 30, 89, 107;
    20th Congress, 108-111, 114,
        116, 152;
    21st, 118;
    22nd, 120 passim; 132, 133;
    27th, 154-58, 162;
    28th, 171;
    growth in members, 129-30;
    trusted, 175; banned, 179
*Contribution to the Critique
    of Political Economy*, 33, 34
*Critique of the Gotha
    Programme*, 50, 120
Davidow, Mike, 15
Dobb, Maurice, 77, 78, 79
German Ideology, 55, 176
Gorbachev, Mikhail, 29, 47,
    158, 159, 161, 164–170,
    171, 172, 175, 180
Hall, Gus, 15, 44–45,163, 169-70
historical materialism, 43, 46–54
Khrushchev, Nikita, 47, 116, 126, 131
Kianouri, Noureddin, 15
Lenin, V. 1., 29, 30, 38, 40, 57, 63,
    72, 77, 143 179; on the Com-
    munist Party, 59, 61; on dem-
    ocracy, 63-65; on the State, 58,
    63-65; on War Communism,
    80-81; on the working class, 60-61;
    theory of imperialism attacked,
    162
Lygachev, Igor, 171, 173, 177
    quoted, 171-72
"Maoism," 141
Menshikov, Stanislav, 162

"New Thinking," 159, 162, 168,
    174-79
Perlo, Victor, 103, 155, 160
Popov, Gavril, attacks theory of
    surplus value, 162
Preobrazhenski, I. A., 86, 89
Ryzhkov, Nikolai, 161
"scissors crisis," 84
Shanin, Lev, 86-7
Stalin, Joseph, 30, 47, 108-10;
    on rapid industrialization, 89;
    on wage equalization, 90-91
"Stalinism," 30, 36, 160
Shevardnadze, Eduard, 162, 180
United Nations, 24, 29
wages, under socialism, 52–54,
    78–79, 90–94, 106, 107, 111–
    117, 119, 121, 149, 155-156
Yakovlev, Alexander, 180
Yeltsin, Boris, 169, 180